REGRESSION OF A NASA WHISTLEBLOWER

SELECTIONS FROM A REGRESSION SESSION WITH COMMENTARY

By Ken Johnston Sr

Editing and Layout
by Karen Christine Patrick

Transcript and Cover Art
by Bret Colin Sheppard

This book is dedicated to my Dad.

Also, to my children,
and their children's children, and beyond,
that they may know the love
and dreams that brought them
into this world.

TABLE OF CONTENTS

FOREWORD

By Karen Christine Patrick, Editor

A MEETING OF MINDS

I was elated when realizing that two people I had worked with, an experienced regression therapist and a unique experiencer, were both at the same place at the same time and available for a hypnotic regression session that is the basis for this book. The story is that Ken finally shares his paranormal experiences. He has been concerned about the "right time" to share this aspect of his life, but now so many have come out with their stories, including experiencers in all realms of science, the aerospace industry, first responders, and people from all walks of life.

My name is Karen Christine Patrick, and I am an experiencer and researcher in UFOs and those who have had contact, a radio producer on the Aquarian Radio Network, and author of the book "The Annunaki and the Moon." I had the privilege of getting to know Ken Johnston Sr while assisting him in getting books and other media out about his extraordinary experiences as part of what he calls his "A-Team" comprising Ken, myself, and my partner, Bret Colin

Sheppard. Bret Sheppard is the author of "Digital Moon," and "Flyover Tsiokolvsky Crater" and the founder of the Lunar Anomaly Research Society, my life, and research partner.

It all happened at a yearly UFO Conference in February of 2016. I had traveled there with Ken Johnston Sr, a whistleblower of NASA image and film manipulations, and Geoff Jordan, a good friend, conference attendee, who became the videographer of this regression event. I was excited to meet my friends and colleagues Dr. Sasha Lessin and his wife Janet Kira Lessin at the conference.

The Lessins are a husband and wife team of therapists who have worked with thousands of experiencers, helping individuals to access sublimated memories. One of our other research friends and a co-host on the Aquarian Radio Network, Reverend John Polk, has an apt term for these memory difficulties, "Alien Anesthesia," a condition that commonly occurs with experiencers encountering otherworldly beings and paranormal experiences.

The Lessins also have many outlets for their research, books and the Aquarian Radio Network. I have been a co-host on the network with Janet for over three years now. We have been interviewing contactees and experiencers, many of whom also have books and other projects out related to their experiences. It's noteworthy how many experiencers also have become healers and teach meditation.

A few have had frightening encounters, but many have gotten messages that are positive, and this correlates with an extensive survey study that was done by the Dr. Edgar Mitchell Foundation for Extraterrestrial Encounters or FREE. UFO conferences and events have become sort of a "family reunion" for those of us touched by the idea that we are not alone in the universe and that there is more to the human story than the consensus reality we are asked to believe.

Having this "Eureka" moment of getting the idea to have Ken get a regression therapy session with Dr. Lessin and Janet had come from the process of working with Ken for several years. My partner, Bret, and I were helping him, requiring extensive questioning for our understanding. For Ken, it meant a lot of remembering and re-connecting the dots of his experience over his lifetime. I was hoping some new information would come out in the regression or some clarification of particular events.

Ken worked at NASA under contract in several capacities. Several odd happenings occurred when he worked in the Data and Photo Control Department of the Lunar Receiving Lab at NASA, where he was handling pictures and film of the moon landings, starting with the first mission that landed on the moon, Apollo 11. Several things happened that made Ken suspicious that something was going on behind the scenes that a faction of the covert realm would never reveal to the public.

THE EXPERIENCER PATH TO DISCLOSURE

For the sake of continuity and control, our society organizes itself, constructs its belief systems, using an "overt and covert" compartmentalization matrix to influence adoption of an agreed-upon set of ideas. Called by some researchers a "consensus reality," its an enforced hierarchical construct that internalizes a state of mind showing us how to interact with it. In recent years, I've been calling this system the "Consensus Reality Show" because the primary means to convey this reality bubble is through media.

We are entangled with the ultimate media machine, being influenced to invest more and more hours accessing each other and all information with a media-based "cloud" via devices. The underlying assumption is that this system will give us a sense of security and mutual understanding to have a cohesive civilization. In this context, "paranormal" is in contrast to what we consider "normal" which is just a statistical range in the famous "Bell Curve" configuration.

For example, in the case of this following graph, a study of youth affiliation behaviors in 1955, we see how the study defined "normal." Incidentally, my father was in the "John Birch" category, so by this study, his affiliation would not be considered "normal." Considering that I grew up "2nd generation conspiracy theorist," exposed to alternative ideas, I definitely didn't feel my upbringing was "normal" but has been quite informative.

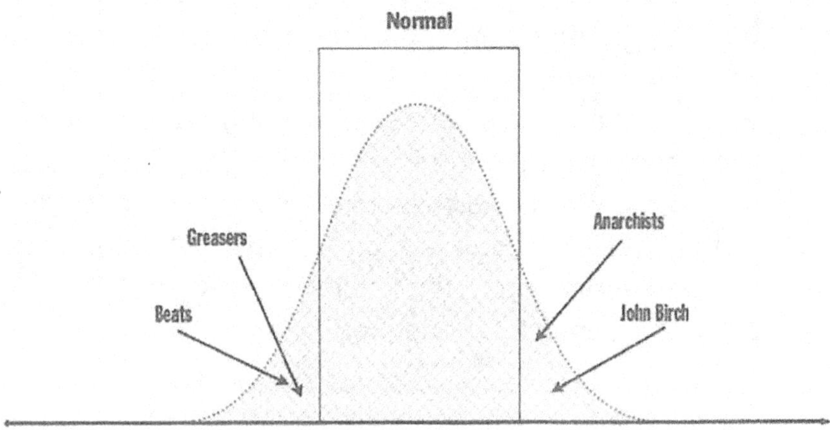

In 1955, the distribution of behaviors was tightly grouped

What we call "normal" falls into a certain range on this curve, introduced to us mostly through childhood assessments in school, i.e., "grading on the curve." Defining "paranormal" or "abnormal" concerns the area not in the center part of the curve.

The definition of paranormal is "denoting events or phenomena such as telekinesis or clairvoyance that are beyond the scope of normal scientific understanding."

This graph applied to human experience might be helpful in determining aggregate experiences but is limited to just these norms. This measure of the psyche of humankind has so ingrained itself, we often ask ourselves, "Is this Normal?" or "Am I Normal?" Maybe my observation is skewed because I seek people who want to talk about unusual experiences, but I think relegating to the categories of "paranormal"

what are misunderstood NORMAL events is harmful,
having put taboos around talking about them openly.

Some extreme experiences may not happen to
everyone, yet are part of all human experiences, such
as war, family tragedy, disability, loss of all kinds. We
would not brand these as "paranormal" although many
can be life-altering. I don't believe it is helpful to
suppress contact experiences, either.

I have been spending more time in the last few years
talking to experiencers one-on-one and interviewing
many on the radio, the last few years with Janet Kira
Lessin and Reverend John Polk. We had a show on
Friday nights, on the Aquarian Radio Network, called
"The Experiencer Path" and I so appreciate the guests
we had, baring their souls and sharing their stories.

Also, at conferences, events, and by phone or internet,
I have been able to have extensive conversations with
quite a few people who are trying to make sense of
what they have experienced. These are just
conversations, some even in front of a communal fire,
a way humans have sorted out the meaning of
everything since the dawn of time.

When somebody tells me their story, I feel blessed to
hear, "You are the first person who I have told this to."
For the experiencer, the path is lonely, denied the
simple human act of being heard and accepted. I
believe the ET visitor's protocol of the "Experiencer

Path" to disclosure, as seen in the pattern of contact, is the way they have chosen to help us overcome hierarchical thinking that allows just a small cadre of folks with control issues to define everyone's experiences.

Unlike some researchers, I think a wide variety of means are being used to contact many individuals. Not just a few, but millions of people throughout many centuries have been experiencers of the otherworldly. When our ancestors were talking about gods and goddesses, star brothers and sisters, the fairy folk or the djinn, or about fantastical beings of all descriptions, I think we should give them the respect that they were talking about authentic experiences in parallel with those of modern times and everyday people.

One exercise I have used to understand more is to "look through the eyes" of our visitors, to see from their point of view. It is a sobering perspective considering all kinds of evils we let run amok and turn a blind eye to, such as human trafficking. Looking at humanity from a planetary observer point of view is also shocking considering the way we use planetary resources.

Many experiencers and contactees are getting messages of concern just about that factor alone from otherworldly beings. The theme of the movie, "The Day the Earth Stood Still" was all about this.

Ours is not likely to be the first civilization found by intergalactic beings to be in such a state of denial. We are a hierarchically-controlled world with a pyramid structure that benefits the few over the many. This situation would seem a barbaric and self-destructive way to live. Observing the arrangement, these visitors may have tried "Take me to your leader" only to have their messages of peace ignored and gifts of technology weaponized.

I imagine that these visitors, if they are kindly, have protocols to assist a hierarchical world system by going directly to the population, in a subtle approach. Not abridging the free will of sentient beings but by carefully exposing information to receptive, psychic, sensitive, intuitive, individuals in the population with new information that would upgrade working philosophies of life, science, and spirituality.

As more and more individuals can absorb and process this information, they will begin to see the illogical base lie assumptions of the current system. As ideas coming into our collective awareness are recognized as more heart-coherent, holistic, and sustainable, they could permeate toward a critical mass that eventually changes the system.

Just accepting that we are not alone in this universe is paradigm-shifting, though threatening to a system that tries to both control the masses but also convince us that theirs is the only way. These are the ones who benefit most from the current paradigm at the expense of everyone else.

I think that what the elite are afraid of is "comparative anthropology" such as comes when a person in a repressed part of the world goes to a more open society and can see how things are done differently. I've talked for several years on the radio about the "Experiencer Path to Disclosure" which I think describes the protocol in play on Earth. The hierarchists still want to control the roll-out of disclosure, dictating that disclosure most not upset what they consider the "natural order," or that the global oligarchy stays in charge.

A story of the "minority report" kind, like Ken's, my own, and others represent an alternative path to disclosure, addressing the "plot-holes" in the story of NASA and other space agencies. Those in charge of this narrative want nothing less than to define True Space to us, and by that, our cosmos and our reality without regard to our values and aspirations. They want to hide that millions don't just "believe" but already know we live in a populated universe, a Paradigm Galactic.

It seems the question we get from readers of Ken's books is that they want to know if we even went to the moon at all. The answer is a "complexity" that misdirects. Ken states that we did go to the moon in the Apollo Era, but we are not told what was found there. Perhaps what was seen and heard was so shocking that a mass campaign of manipulation of the information, the photo and film evidence, the narrative, was instituted to cover up the real story.

It has been an insightful journey working with Ken Johnston Sr these last few years. It is hard to fathom that an event unfolded from 50 years ago, still has yet to be told and fully understood. I am especially proud to have worked on this book chronicling Ken's candid testimony.

Every year, we lose the witnesses to history during our overt manned missions to the moon. Many have made statements over the years of what they saw and heard that differed from the official narrative. Millions of people who are younger have now taken an interest and need to know the underlying story. I believe what compels them to look into the alternate views is because of their own experiences.

It is my philosophy to respect the stories of my elders and ancestors and to keep faith with those who have gone on before. We need to learn history as it indeed was, to hear a diversity of voices, and not let an entrenched hierarchy dominate the narrative if it means that the results are less than humane and uninspiring.

Better to hear the authentic story, much more weird, much more astounding, and infinitely more inspiring. When we look back with clarity, we can define a coherent present moment, thus choose a positive future for a world that works for everybody.

Peace is not a lull between bomb blasts. But to envision the world that Beckwith and others at the conference invoked — to compress hope into a rending certainty that such a world is possible as well as necessary peels away the numbness and cynicism that lets us live in this one. No wonder so few people are embracing it.

And yet that's not true at all. A yearning for peace is at everyone's core, and the recognition of our complex, planetary interdependence is hardly controversial. Peace studies and nonviolent conflict resolution — the technology of peace — are gaining prominence in universities around the world.

"There are new ideas on the world's horizon, as different from the twentieth-century worldview as the twentieth century was different from the nineteenth century," writes Marianne Williamson, founder of the Peace Alliance, in her book Healing the Soul of America. "We are ready to apply principles of healing and recovery, not just to our bodies, not just to our relationships, but to every aspect of life."

~ From "A World That Works For Everybody"
by Robert-Koehler
https://www.huffingtonpost.com/robert-koehler/
a-world-that-works-for-ev_b_40694.html

INTRODUCTION

By Ken Johnston Sr, Author

This book is based on actual events.

My journey of self-awareness was a difficult and emotional road to travel. Loaded with some of the more subtle mysteries of one's life, some of which I could only describe as a surprise. One of my realizations came early on, with the acknowledgment of my dyslexia, I believe I'm only 57 years old, of course, I will let the readers figure that out for themselves.

I realize as well we have lived many lifetimes for which few can remember unless under hypnosis. Also for me as well, the discovery of new surprising knowledge of my past lives or parallel lives.

There are many childhood memories that don't make too much sense, but later in life, we realize how meaningful they can be. I believe now it is crucial to recover and overcome some of those problematic memories as well as the pleasant ones if one is to become self-aware about their place in this world. Nothing is an accident.

I believe each of us has a purpose in life that effects the world.

We all have or will experience a profound sense of our existence, and when that happens, it is marvelous, a freeing moment in time. I share my experiences with the world regarding my involvement with the Apollo program at NASA JPL, and now my life regression.

CHAPTER 1

<u>FRAN AND ME</u>

WORKING IN THE SPACE SHUTTLE PROGRAM

Before December in 1980, I had accepted a position with the Martin Marietta Corporation in Denver Colorado, to go to work for them on the Space Shuttle Program. The first part would be the approach and landing tests so that we could establish the right procedures.

Martin Marietta sent a team of us to Vandenberg Air Force base just south of Santa Maria, California. Once we were there, the objective was to make preparations for a program designated as the "Slick-Six Launch Facility." Which was Designed for launching ICBM's (Intercontinental Ballistic Missiles) off the West Coast, now the facility was to serve the Space Shuttle Program.

The team's job was to redesign the launch facilities to make it possible to launch the Space Shuttle from the west coast. While we were converting Slick-Six, I was up for recommendation by some of the Apollo Astronauts to be on the next Space shuttle flight, but NASA decided they wanted astronauts that were scientists and those with specialty degrees, so my opportunity as a NASA Astronaut ended right there.

The Space Shuttle designated as Challenger was launched at Cape Canaveral Florida and exploded before it could reach orbit. We lost all seven of the Astronauts on board, including the one civilian school teacher. It was a shocking and tragic event for the whole country. All the people who had worked on the project were also sad for the families who lost loved ones that day.

While I was packed up and ready to go to Florida and the launch facility there as I had been re-assigned, instead, because of the disaster, NASA canceled the West Coast Space Shuttle program and began closing down the Slick Six facility on the west coast.

It was also after the Challenger disaster that Martin Marietta laid off a large group of engineers under a reduction in force (RIF), and I was out of work again, in-between contracts, typical of this industry. Also at this time, I had divorced and become a single dad.

I went back to Houston, Texas for a brief time to work with my brother Dr. A.R. Johnston on repairing Yachts after a series of hurricanes came through and destroyed thousands of boats along the Gulf, in Galveston and Houston, Texas.

A.R. had formed the JAMAR boat company. When I arrived, I parked my van inside the big boathouse and started working to design and repair these elegant boats that had holes the size of a Volkswagen "Bug" in some of them.

A.R. designated me as the CFO (Chief Financial Officer) of JAMAR. I did such a good job that I soon worked myself out of being needed. I suggested to my brother, that instead of paying me the salary of the CFO to just hire a clerk or bookkeeper to maintain the files. I then received the offer to go work for Boeing in Seattle, so I packed up and took my son Michael to the west coast. We stopped by Santa Maria, and I left him with his mother so that he could finish high school and so that I could head up to Seattle, WA for work.

At Boeing, I started my job as a Human Factors Engineer. I went back to work at the Boeing 737 flight training school and ended up working there for the next fourteen years as a 737 flight instructor. I had many rewarding experiences with students from all over the world.

One of the most exciting experiences I had there was when we taught the Chinese students how to fly the 737. The first group that came to Seattle had the director of the CAAC (Chinese Aviation Organization) the equivalent of the FAA (Federal Aviation Administration) in the U.S.

We were on break one day, and the director had his translator talking with me, and asked me how I liked working with people from other countries with a variety of languages? I looked at him and looked at the translator and told him, "Do the best you can and translate this word for word." I said, "I like everybody. I don't care what their race, religion, creed, or color is.

But I don't like assholes no matter what their race, religion, creed, or color is." After that, the director acknowledged an understanding and gave me a big bear hug, and said, "We would have been friends where ever we met." And that is my philosophy, I like everybody no matter where they are from, and enjoy the diversity of other cultures. I enjoyed the rest of my career with Boeing as a flight instructor.

MEETING FRAN

Some of my coworkers there in Seattle suggested that if I wanted a nightlife and to have a little fun, to check out Parents Without Partners (PWP). So I did just that, and went one evening to dance and socialize. So it was just what it says, "Parents Without Partners," putting on a big dance every Friday night, the opportunity to meet people of the opposite sex, and who knows, one thing might lead to another. I thought it would be a great idea to dress up special and put on a nice three-piece suit, shave, and put on some nice cologne, and go to my first PWP dance.

No sooner than I had walked through the front door and paid my fee, one of the older ladies said, "Oh I've just the right person for you to meet." She took me into the dance hall and over to a table and pointed out Fran. She said, "Fran, I'd like for you to meet Ken Johnston." Not use to being a single man, I looked at Fran and said, "I bet you're wondering what a guy like me is doing in a place like this." She replied, "No not really." My first impression was not exactly what I wanted it to be, yes, perhaps I was a bit nervous as it felt similar to a job interview, but we sat and talked, danced and visited.

We just hit it off instantly and liked one another, so we started dating outside of the PWP events. Fran was the Administrative Assistant to the Vice President of the Solar Department of the Boeing company, in charge of Solar wind technology all over the world. She was making good money and doing quite well, raising two little girls ages 8 and 10. That would be Deanna the oldest and Caroline being the youngest. After Fran and I dated for a month and a half, Boeing was going to send me to Vandenberg Air Force base, back in Santa Maria California to begin work on the Peacekeeper missile system.

I discussed everything with Fran and told her that I would love for her to go with me, but we couldn't go in the same status that we were. I paused, and she said,

"Well, if you were asking me to marry you, I would have to think about it." I said, "Well, this is Wednesday, and we would have to be married by this weekend so that Boeing could give us the orders to ship both of us down to Santa Maria." So I said "What would be your answer, if you had thought about it for a while?" and she said, "Well, it would be YES!"

In three days, we put together a beautiful formal wedding, and I have some beautiful pictures of Fran and her two little girls that stood up with us as we got married. The minister, in fact, turned to the girls and said, "Do you take this man to be your dad?" And both girls said YES!!. That was the beginning of thirty-three years of our happy marriage, not that we haven't had a lot of challenges and curve balls along the way, but we always work together on any obstacles that were in our way.

Once we got to Santa Maria, no sooner did we get there we found a place to rent, my two boys, who were living with their mother not far, decided to move in with Fran and me, and their new little sisters. The situation was challenging, to say the least, for Fran now had two teenage boys to take care of as well, but like always, we worked together. We can look back at it thirty-three years later and say none of that was an accident when considering the chances of the probability of Fran and me meeting.

Fran was born outside of Vancouver, Canada, on one of the logging ranges. She has a dramatic story to tell about things that happened in her life before we met. Her father and two younger brothers were killed in a boating accident, and she still had two younger brothers, as she had to grow up taking care of them.

Later, she would leave in a marriage that didn't work out with an abusive man, with an incredible journey of emigrating from Canada and winding up down in Seattle, Washington.

She got a job at the Boeing Company and working her way up the ladder into a good position. Then we ended up together. The chances are astronomical that we met, as I was way down in Houston during those times, yet winding up there in Seattle by some fateful turn of events.

INCIDENT AT VANDENBERG AIR FORCE BASE

While Fran and I were in Santa Maria, I was contracted out for the Boeing Company at Vandenberg as a human factors engineer. One of the things that we had to do was to dress up in protective clothing and wore headsets because we were within a mile of the launch silos.

The U.S. was testing out International Continental Ballistic Missiles like the Peacekeeper missile. We would say, "You know how you keep peace in the world? It's whoever has the biggest club, gets to declare peace." I was working on a team that had the missile that could not only go into orbit but could also send down around eight warheads or directed hits on a given target. Remember now this was at the time of the Cold War.

We were trying to keep the U.S. and Russia from entering into a nuclear war by showing that the other had more or equal firepower, a policy called M.A.D. Or "mutually assured destruction." All the personnel there were under orders never to discuss anything outside of work and some cases not even to the other departments.

I remember one particular event when we were having dinner, and one of the people next to us said, "Oh yeah, do you remember Mary Sue? That she was doing this and that with the company?" We noticed that others at different tables were leaning in trying to eavesdrop because every major company out of Japan, China, Germany, and Russia had represent- atives out to spy on personnel from Vandenberg.

I recall a strange event that happened there while testing the Peacekeeper. It occurred when we were out on site about a mile away from the launch silo. Something we watched for, while observing a missile launch from the silo was the shielding on the sides of the missile that could peel off and fall to earth.

The amount of vibration and noise created when your that close is very loud. Being in that environment is most likely where I developed some hearing loss as one's whole body vibrated when these things launched.

After one of these launches, we gathered back in the facility office and reviewed the videos of the day's launch. The Peacekeeper missile was climbing up in altitude changing its orbit to be more of a polar orbit, from north to south instead of east to west. As we watched the missile climbing up on the video, an unknown glowing craft overtook it at over fifty thousand feet.

The UFO moved in close to the warhead of the missile, both visible in the film. The small craft sent a beam striking the warhead, then went around to the other side at incredible speed shooting another beam at the missile again. Afterwards, the UFO took off quickly and disappeared, and the missile tumbled out of control, then exploded, the debris falling back to Earth.

It's anyone's guess what could outrun a Peacekeeper ICBM disabling it. What it seems is that both Russia and the U.S. are monitored by extraterrestrials to keep us from blowing ourselves up. This incident was also reported by Professor Robert Jacobs, USAF Lieutenant retired and later verified with a letter from his SCD in charge at the time F.J. "Sonny" Mansmann. Capt. Robert Salas also speaks of these similar craft landing by other missile silos and disabling missiles before they were even off the ground.

One of the other things that happened while we were at Vandenberg working on the Peacekeeper was that we went down underground to the mission control center rooms and these were between sixty and a hundred feet deep underground. Supposedly, we would be safe in the event of a nuclear attack. If we were attacked, it would be like taking the whole underground room and suspending it a hundred feet in the air. In other words, it was a false sense of security and wasn't safe at all even though it had three-foot thick steel doors going into the launch control room underground.

We thought we were safe in the event of a direct hit, then found out that there was no way we would have survived inside that observation gondola, because the impact from such a weapon would create a crater hundreds of feet deep, and thousands of feet wide.

BACK TO SEATTLE

After we finished the launch testing of the Peacekeeper missile for Boeing, they sent us back to Seattle where we found an apartment, and I was very fortunate, because I was a pilot and had the prior training experience, to get another job with the flight training department there on the aviation side. I became one of the flight instructors for the Boeing 737 which happened to be, and still is, one of the most popular and in-demand commercial aircraft used for both corporate and passenger planes. It is also one of the most efficient aircraft in use around the world. That's how I wound up back in Seattle Washington with Fran and the two girls.

Both boys stayed in Santa Maria, California. As soon as Ken Jr. graduated, he went to school at Cal Tech, and Michael came with me in the camper trailer to Seattle when Boeing helped us move all our stuff back up to Seattle.

The place we moved to just happened to be next to a place that had some horses. Horses had always been Fran's dream and love. She had a horse when she was a teenager, had bought it herself and took care of it. Her mother eventually had her sell it. My wife has always been a lover of horses. We rented a few weeks there until we found a home out in Kent, Washington. Not long after we got there, we got our first horse, and we lived there for the next several years while we were working at the Boeing Company.

After working at Boeing for years in the flight training department, about 1995, the economy was taking a turn for the worse. Boeing offered an early retirement plan for those of us that had put in more than ten years. At the time, Boeing sold the training flight crew department to an independent flight training corporation which resulted in political challenges there, and the tension was palpable. Finally, my wife said that she wanted me around a lot longer and to take the retirement from Boeing. We looked at our possibilities and what we should do at this time.

ON TO NEW MEXICO

Fran had taken on some independent contractor work, and had also left her career with Boeing. She was also in communication with the Bureau of Indian Affairs since we both have a Native American history and background. The tribes were looking for someone to come to Albuquerque (ABQ), NM and work for the Bureau of Indian Affairs (BIA). She accepted the position, and we moved the whole family to New Mexico.

We had some friends of ours that told us about a place that used to be a monastery for Catholic monks, and we moved in. So I retired, became a "house husband," with Fran as the primary breadwinner. After living in ABQ for some time. This particular house was known for having some strange things take place. Fortunately, Fran and I have a history of such experiences; we think ghosts seem to like us. Friends would visit, be in the house no more than fifteen minutes, and they would get very nervous and want to leave immediately after feeling some strange vibes.

Eventually, we found a home in Belen, New Mexico and have been there for eighteen years. We have just less than three acres, and Fran wanted to get some horses again because that is her passion. We ran into to someone down the road that was raising miniature horses. I went over and checked them out, brought information back, sat down with Fran at the dinner table, and showed her what miniature horses are. Doing a bit of research, I found that miniature horses were usually bred for the Royalty in Europe and England for the children of Kings and Queens. They are different from Shetland ponies and are small, but fully-proportional horses.

At the end of World War One (WWI), America sent one of their top coal miners to England to find out how they did their coal mining. The gentleman was looking down at the mine and saw all these miniature horses pulling the wagons of coal. He thought that was a great idea so he bought a whole herd of miniature horses and brought them back to the U.S. so they could also use them for mining. Many of the horses used were born raised, lived, and died underground in the mines.

After electric motors were developed and stronger than the miniature horses, they brought the horses back up out of the underworld to live on the surface, and they have been making quite the comeback. Their history is very colorful. When King Henry found out that the Dukes and Duchesses were getting these horses, he made a law that they get war horses or face execution. The miniature breeds almost became extinct in Europe after the invention of electric motors. Through the past seventeen years that we have lived here in Belen, my wife has been raising them and breeding miniature horses, including producing national champions.

Recently, we went to a national miniature horse show where one of Fran's horses won grand champion. I think that speaks well for her and the little horses she has taken care of all these years.

We are still married with 18 grandchildren and even three great-grandchildren. It is a miracle how the impossible can sometimes come true. I LOVE YOU, FRAN!!

CHAPTER 2

THE A-TEAM WORKING

MEETING BRET SHEPPARD AND KAREN PATRICK

For years I had been thinking about writing a book about my life, the space program, and strange things that had happened to me throughout my life. I covered most of that in my autobiography. After the completion of that book, I wanted to also talk about the possibility that I was contacted by extraterrestrial beings and even abducted by them for some future purpose. But before the first book was published, I made contact with some people that made the idea of writing some books possible.

One night, while I was at home at my computer chatting away with people about my time with the Apollo Moon program and how I had saved an archive of pictures, slides, and film from the Moon program, an interesting fellow challenged me to prove that this archive, in fact, existed. I found myself chatting with a gentleman named Bret Sheppard, the founder of the Lunar Anomaly Research Society. I had been looking at the discussions by members of the group on

Facebook, and Bret and I were discussing some of the anomalies in some of the pictures in the archive. The next thing you know we were exchanging scanned pictures from each of our collections and this fellow knew his stuff. I was impressed.

We discussed the idea of Bret and his partner, Karen Christine Patrick helping me with getting the archive out on the internet in some way. I found out that Bret's family, Karen and Bret's daughter, Cheyenne Sheppard, lived in Texarkana, Texas and were preparing to move to the Washington State so that Karen could live closer to her family.

The only problem was that their van, that they planned to move with had stopped running and the mechanic was refusing to return it to them unless he got the job to fix it and charge them an "arm and a leg" for doing it. Apparently, this crooked mechanic had a history of doing this to stranded motorists.

The police wouldn't do anything about it. Bret and Karen were at a point that they were considering just leaving everything they had in the home they were renting, take the bus, and leave everything behind.

Suddenly, I felt this overwhelming feeling to tell them that there was another option! I said to them that I had a good Ford F-150 pickup and a 16-foot, flatbed trailer and I could come and get them. That way they could keep all the furniture and belongings. Bret had also been asking me so many questions about my archive and stopping where I lived would allow him to see it.

I did also want to ask for help with a book or a website since they had those abilities. It was a 777-mile one-way trip, and 14 hours later I was there. The family was packed, and we started loading almost immediately. An hour later we pulled away from Texarkana and headed WEST!!

The rest of the trip was quite an adventure. Bret and I took turns driving. Providentially, we made a wrong turn and almost went to Dallas. The tarp I had brought was old and shredded, so we took it off, with all their belongings now exposed to the weather. Because we got temporarily lost, we avoided a thunderstorm. Somebody was watching over us all.

Beloved family members, Brigette and Brianna, two rescue hound dogs that Bret had raised from puppies, had never been out of their backyard. Suddenly, were put in a crate for safety and put into the back of my truck. They must have thought they had been abducted by aliens. Missing that thunderstorm also was a blessing for Brigette, as she is very afraid of storms. After that trip, it took awhile for them to recover as the frisky, friendly dogs they usually are.

When we course-corrected, we headed back North to pick up with Interstate 40. Right at that point, we had to stop. We parked in a Walmart parking lot, refreshed the dogs, and all took a nap in the truck. Two hours later we started again and stopped for breakfast. Our bodies needed a little refreshment.

During this time, Karen was looking at possible places to rent in Washington. There is quite the difference between rents in New Mexico and those in Washington. Since the family decided to try and move on this particular trip, the rents in Washington were going up. The fact of this figures into what happened right after the trip.

Thirty-six hours after I started this trip, we pulled into the driveway of my house. Next, we made a couple of calls and found a storage place where we could unload the trailer. It was Sunday, so we rested.

Bret and Karen finally had a chance to see the archive. They were stunned and amazed, as Richard Hoagland and his "people" had been years ago. They realized there was a research opportunity here to help get the archive online to the world and get my story put down in more detail than had been done before.

Sunday night, Bret and Karen, discussing it with Cheyenne, decided to stay in Belen, New Mexico for a year and dig into the story. They now also wanted to watch the real estate situation in Washington State to see if the rental costs were going to continue to rise, making it more difficult for them to relocate.

Monday we located an apartment in downtown Belen, loaded up all their belongings, and moved them into a new place to live for a while. They stayed in Belen for two years, actually, finding New Mexico to be a great "hub" kind of place for research and to attend conference events that convene about the anomaly, paranormal, and UFO topics. Since Bret and Karen moved to New Mexico, the three of us have been to quite a few events together, as I dubbed it the "A-Team."

They lived downtown for a year, then moved to a place with a view of the mountains, near the Belen Municipal Airport which was up on the West Mesa. To the West and South are mountains and to the East is the Rio Grande Valley. Driving down from the mesa, it's a great view of the small town of Belen, population 5,500, further to the East are the Manzano Mountains. North, about 45 minutes away is Albuquerque, and Karen got excited listening to the radio one day and hearing a car commercial from a dealer in Roswell. Yes, we are that close to the UFO capital of the world, just a few hours drive away.

Finding a home in New Mexico permanently, the family lived there for two years, then moved to Silver City, New Mexico, where they can participate in the art scene there and create a yearly anomaly conference. Bret and Karen have been able to travel to the Pacific Northwest to see the family since then, finding the weather here nice to come home to.

As the A-Team got busy, we worked on the book "KEN'S MOON: Revealing the 'Dark Mission' of

NASA." This book was an autobiography. Bret used scans of many of the pictures from the archive and from my collection of Mission Reports to create two e-books that we shared with people that first year. Later, Bret decided to re-scan all the pictures in the archive, it is now online at Archive.org, a site with a huge amount of information from all over the internet. By putting it online, the pictures could be a much higher resolution.

Anomaly hunters value the archive as an alternative to the digitized images on NASA which have been processed digitally to the extent that anomalies and the image numbers are not right on there as in my collection. Bret's study of image manipulation digitally has resulted in a book that he wrote, "DIGITAL MOON" by Bret Colin Sheppard.

GOING TO SCOTTSDALE, ARIZONA

In 2016, Karen contacted some dear friends of hers, Dr. Sasha and Janet Lessin, that were going to attend the next International UFO Congress that was going to be in Scottsdale, Arizona in February. They offered us the opportunity to use a part of their booth to sell the digital copies of the archive, an early scan edition.

In the meantime, as we prepared to go to the event, I had become 'internet friends' with a fellow named Geoff Jordan. Geoff worked for a railroad company as an Engineer, and he was a fan of my work. We became good friends over the internet. When we told him that we were going to attend the UFO Congress, he said that he wanted to come down and pick us up in his Winnebago RV and take us to the Congress so we would have lodging. Geoff came to Belen and also got to see the archive, as so many have.

Bret stayed home with the dogs and such, so Karen and I loaded up what we needed for the conference and away we went. I took my truck because of another speaking event that I had to come back for a little early. So I just followed Geoff and Karen all the way to Scottsdale, Arizona. We pulled into the parking lot of the Hotel and made a home for the next four days.

We went into the conference center and located Dr. Sasha Lessin and his wife, Janet. We have met people such as Sasha and Janet Lessin who are very well-known, and well-thought-of in the UFO and ET community for their Annunaki studies, as well as Sasha, being a professional therapist and hypnotist.

As things turned out, I was not allowed to use a part of the table that Janet Lessin was taking care of. It seems that the owner of the table was not all that friendly. Well, two days later, after she realized that I was the guy that had saved all those awesome pictures of the Moon, she just had to have me on her radio program.

Not being tied down to a booth proved very advantageous. I met many more people that way,

walking around and meeting people. I carried a 24" by
X 40" poster of a base on the moon discovered by Bret
that was visible on one of my pictures from my archive.
People would stop me and ask questions and I would
answer them and tell them that I had published my
CD's and they could have them for a very low price.
The CD had an early version of my first book, the
autobiography now at KenJohnstonMedia.net.

We made enough money to pay for the expenses for
our first A-Team venture into the UFO conventions. I
enjoyed meeting people, many of whom knew
something about my story. Later in the event, Frank
Jacob and Tonia Madenford, producers of the movie.
"Packing for Mars," let me hang out at their booth.

That is a great documentary about how we may have
secretly gone to Mars back in the day. Our space
program was tracking towards a manned trip to Mars
after Apollo, slated for the 1970s, but we stopped
going beyond Near-Earth orbit after Apollo 17.

Featured in "Packing for Mars" was Andrew Basiago,
"Chrononaut" and participant in the "Jumproom"
program. I have since met Andy, had long chats with
him and got the scoop on covert space activities that
happened after Apollo.

I was excited to find out that the possibility exists that
we may have gone to Mars in a Secret Space
Program. America abandoning dreams of space had
mystified me, especially seeing how hard we worked

to get there when I worked at NASA. I have a strong affinity for Mars and would go right now if they let me.

Karen introduced me to Dr. And Mrs Lessin and it became a possibility to have the regression session with them that is the basis for this book. While visiting with Dr. Sasha Lessin, I learned that he was a professional Hypnotist as well as a Psychologist. I told him a lot about my childhood and the types of alien contact that had happened throughout my life. We agreed to explore events from my childhood up to the present time. The Lessins had conducted sessions with hundreds of experiencers, so I felt very comfortable with the idea.

The session happened in the hotel room with the Lessins, Karen was there and left to "man" the book-selling booth for the Sasha and Janet Lessin during the regression, Geoff Jordan was there as the videographer. The audio from the session was transcribed by Bret Sheppard and has been edited for this book by Karen Patrick. I appreciate all the help from everybody to make this all possible.

Much more happened at that event, and the A-Team had a busy time since I met Bret and Karen online three years ago at the writing of this book.

ON TO ROSWELL

The A-Team's next venture was to attend the UFO Festival in Roswell, New Mexico during the July 4th weekend of that year. We had a table at the Roswell UFO Museum and Research Center, and Bret and I got to speak several times there. Also, Bret and I got to ride on the float at the night-time parade. The Roswell event is really fun and family-friendly.

I have been able to also speak at several MUFON (Mutual UFO Network) meetings, other conferences, including the Mars Anomaly Research Society Conference in Mobile Alabama. This year, the M.A.R.S. Conference will be in Silver City, New Mexico.   The word was spreading about the archive and all the evidence I had saved all these years. The truth is getting out.

SETTING THE SCENE OF THE REGRESSION

As I settled in at the regression session in Scottsdale, AZ, in 2016, the question had come up whether or not I had ever been hypnotized, or had done a regression to find out really what all has happened in my youth to my current age. I also wanted to know more about unusual experiences I have had.

I had myself been trained as a hypnotist in my senior year of high school at the Oklahoma Military Academy because of my interest as a child. I got books on hypnotism and studied and was able to work with some of the other cadets there, learning how to put them under hypnosis. To protect myself from being hypnotized without me knowing, I created a keyword.

For self-hypnosis, this was the key I would use to relax myself during meditation.

I would use the same techniques to help others relax and study in school to help them do better on exams. I would use the same techniques later to help some of the graduate students prepare for their tests. More people should explore these techniques to help relax and focus.

I know from experience that hypnosis has great good value but also important that I made sure no one could hypnotize me so easily. People kept asking me from the alternative community, saying you've had all these experiences, why not try regression to see if you can remember more. I had gotten to the point over the years where I would try to keep from remembering things, especially painful memories.

I thought about all that, lying there, getting ready for the regression. I remembered being in a comfortable mood and was ready to begin. I was conscious at the time, but during the regression I didn't remember anything. After the regression, I realized I had been crying, shaking all over. I thought I was only hypnotized and under for fifteen to twenty minutes but was told that actually, I was under for about two and a half hours.

I feel that all my experiences have brought me to this present time, sharing the archive and stories of working in the space program. Now, I am aware of a certain timeline we are on that will bring us into a knowledge of extraterrestrial life, even if certain factions don't want that to happen for some reason. I think our E.T. Visitors want us to know. I want to know.

CHAPTER 3

AN ABUSIVE STEPFATHER

MY FAMILY BACKGROUND COMES INTO PLAY

[Editor's note: comments not in the regression, or as actions within the regression, will be in italics to differentiate background information from the actual happening.]

In 1945 or '46, when I was about three or four, my mother was married to Roger Womeldorf, who was a Marine Corps Captain or Major who had come back from the Guadalcanal with an infection in his ear that leaked to his brain and that the pain was so severe that he committed suicide.

In the recovery from losing my father and her next husband, my mom started going out to the country club to dances and parties and met a gentleman by the name of "T.C. Ray" the name on his birth certificate. When he joined the Army, the Army said you have to have a first name, so they gave him Troy Charles Ray.

So they met and became very close friends, and T.C. had just come back from the battles in Korea. They got married soon after. Shortly after that, we moved from Edmonton to Hart, Texas where T.C. had some land. He had helped my mom get rid of the property that she and her former husband had together. My mom wanted to move to Norman, Oklahoma where her mother, Maggie, my grandma, and the rest of the clan lived. So we moved from Hart, Texas to Norman, Oklahoma.

I was in the third grade at the time, and coming from a small place like Hart, with only five hundred people at the time, and moving to Norman that had the quite large Oklahoma University. It was a huge city and a bit too overwhelming for T.C. completely. His temperament required more of the country life, so we all packed up and moved back to Hart, Texas.

I ended up having to do the third grade over because of the chaotic move. So we were back in Hart, and interacted with the Ray family along with the Hart family were the ones who founded the town of Hart.

My mom became the post Mistresses there, and T.C. became the County Commissioner, so his family was well thought of in the history of the town. But, he had a very sadistic side to him that most people in the town did not know. I don't know if it was due to how he grew up and the way he was treated as a child or what, but he did not like me, a "Momma's boy" or my older brother A.R. because he was too old to be considered a son. But Jimmy, my other brother, was his pride and joy, and T.C. thought of him to inherit the ways of the farm. T.C. would do things like slapping me around, grab my hair and yank me.

He uses to kick me and used a razor strap, the kind that barbers used to shave men, a leather strap to whip the daylights out of me, and it would leave bruises. I had every reason in the world to want to leave and go to a military school. My brother Jimmy was killed on the school hayride when some drunk illegal aliens came around the corner and hit the tractor my brother was on, trapping Jimmy underneath the wheel and he died instantly.

My mother and I went back to visit her mom, my grandma Kratz. Mother met her friend whose son was at the Oklahoma Military Academy. I wanted to enroll and that gave me the opportunity to get away from T.C. and go to military school. It took years and years for me to finally accept the fact that T.C. did step up to the plate taking on all of us boys and my mom.

Willing to marry a woman with three children, and do the best he could at being a stepdad, and I can now forgive him for the things that he did to me, as he did the best that he could. It made me wonder what kind of childhood he may have had. That was a sad side of the story.

The good times I remember later, when I became a stepdad myself, but I couldn't, to this day, conceive of repeating the abuse I suffered as a child. I've worked through it for over thirty years to come to closure, and having those experiences made me who I am today.

Now here is where the regression starts. I went to the hotel room of Dr. Sasha and Janet Lessin, Geoff Jordan is there as the videographer. They were making me comfortable so that I could go under hypnosis.

THE REGRESSION BEGINS

KEN: Gotta adjust the shade, and unscrew the top.

GEOFF JORDAN: Just relax, okay? You're not in charge.

KEN: *(says under his breath)* Oh, jeez. That's true.

JANET LESSIN: Get comfortable. Loosen your jacket.   I'll have the camera ready to just press record when we start.

DR. LESSIN: Just forget all of your preconceived notions about what therapy should be. I'm going to give you some things to work with. Okay, the way we work this is that we see a person full of different aspects.

Ken is a whole person with a lot of different aspects. Ken has one aspect that tells him how to improve his performance, and Ken has another aspect who is an inner child who has to deal with a lot of emotions and Ken's feelings. Ken has a chief commander that knows how to tell other people what to do and when to do it, and so on, and so forth.

Every one of us has multiple sub-personalities, our different aspects. We first must get consent from Ken's prevailing sub-personality, which is more or less like a mixture of intelligence and affability, or somewhere near that analogy.

We need permission from Ken's dominant side so that Ken's different aspects are free to come out if they are needed. But we need to let Ken know that if he begins to feel uncomfortable or feels like it's becoming overwhelming, or at any time it seems things are not in Ken's best interest to go on further. Ken may just interrupt and say, "I don't want to continue this," until we have had a chance to talk about it, to think about it, or whatever.

Ken may want to stop until he can remember the context. There might also be things that Ken feels are just too private to explore. There might be a point where Ken needs to stop everything, and we are letting Ken know that if it comes to that, he may just say, "turn everything off."

KEN: So, if I don't want something recorded, just say, "I don't want to go there?"

DR. LESSIN: Yes, that's right. And at the end, we are going to bring Ken back to the center, where Ken will have all his aspects brought together again. Then, when Ken is together, we will assess the situation and evaluate what the next step is for Ken's best interest. What we do is have Ken move in and out of his whole person by moving to the right or to the left of Ken's whole self. An example of this would be if we want to access Ken's intellect aspect, we would ask Ken to think of physically moving into the intellect embodiment.

When we are in an intellectual realm, we do not allow emotions to freely consume us; we only want to be logical. How does Ken function within the whole system of self, when Ken is in the intellectual mode?

KEN: It depends on whether I'm getting ready to focus on relaxing, I have a meditation that I go through, having to do with protection from psychological outside influences, and once I have cleared those I feel safe and comfortable to relax and go to sleep.

DR. LESSIN: You're saying that when in that mode, the function is to assess whether or not it's okay for you to go into an alpha state? Can you go to Beta, which is an even slower state than alpha?

KEN: It's been a long time since I have, yes, but I could - about forty years ago.

DR. LESSIN: You're the only one who can see the full spectrum concerning your emotions. We want Ken's intellect to know that you alone are the interpreter. If there is a time when Ken needs to slow down and reevaluate more, if he is going somewhere you deem unsafe, just physically move back to the center of the bed, even if that seems like a silly thing to do. Here we go now. Okay, Ken's intellect is over here, but you can mention that you have other ones. You have mentioned all the aspects, and there is a meditative one, also.

Each part has resonance, so there might be something that occurred when you were a kid or something that happened during past lives, and naturally, there will be something that happened that Ken wants to find out more about, a critical incident, that you want to explore in depth and explain in detail, so when the time is right we will ask you to access this part.

Now I will ask you to move around to any space so that we can ask you to move into your inner child. Every one of us is that inner child, and even though you are this great big person, you are this child inside. There is a great big person inside you and a great person inside of us. When you're in that child, he is vulnerable, and he is flooded with emotions.

Ken normally doesn't show that on the outside, I know, he keeps him on the inside. Feelings can get hurt when you are young and emotional. Are you able to get in touch with how it feels when you let the inner child come out? How do you communicate with Ken?

KEN: I feel the frustration, and I feel vulnerable to the attacks.

DR. LESSIN: Yes.

KEN: I want to get out of that environment, and just walk away.

DR. LESSIN: Was there something like that, when you wanted to walk away when you were a kid? Did something happen to make you feel that way?

KEN: With all the stepfathers and things with or another, not that it feels like it affected me.

DR. LESSIN: No, no. First of all, I'm not asking if it affected you. It just sounds like the best thing to do, just put distance between you and the situation.

KEN: I was so small. I didn't have that option then, or control of that authority, because I wasn't in control, and I do like to have control.

DR. LESSIN: Okay. Now, there we are. That is really significant. So you are young and are unable to get away from your stepfather. When you wanted to get away, but couldn't, how did you deal with whatever you couldn't get away from? And what was it that was happening that made you want to just get away from the situation?

KEN: I can recall being wrapped up and being switched with a razor strap, and I struggle and fight to get away until it's over, and I'm just left till he's finished beating me up.

DR. LESSIN: What did you do? How did you handle getting beat-up while he was beating you?

KEN: It was just total fear.

DR. LESSIN: Fear, huh, so you suffered through the years until you were big enough to get away from the situations?
KEN: Yes. And or in my mother's case, she divorced him, and we moved away. She just...

DR. LESSIN: So, the next question would be, what did your mother do when she knew you were getting hit with a razor strap?

KEN: It usually happened when she was not around, and it only happened once or twice. And I would tell my mom, of course. She wound up getting married twelve times to eight different men, so I had many stepfathers at various stages of my life. And about halfway through her selection of "bad apples," she called them, and I said, "So long as you keep picking off the bottom of the barrel, you will find only the bad apples." Once I turned twelve and thirteen, going into

the 9th grade, I went to the Oklahoma Military Academy. Actually, I turned thirteen a month after I got into military school.

DR. LESSIN: Wow, you really did get away. Okay, let's see if I got this straight. In part, some of the reasons why your mother would leave her husbands are because they were mean to you?

KEN: Yes. My brother, who was five years older than me, he had to go live with grandparents, and my brother Jimmy who was 17 months older than me, was my protector in school, so no one messed with me, or else Jimmy would kick their butt. And then, of course, he was killed in an accident while on a school hayride, when I was around 12. Mother had always tried to say she was trying to find a father for us kids, and I told her we didn't need one. She was impressed with that, and I told her she needs to find someone you're happy with. She didn't do good at that either.

DR. LESSIN: Wow! What I'm understanding here is that your Mother was really concerned with your welfare.

KEN: Totally.

DR. LESSIN: And so your mother would not continue to let you be in that situation where you were being beaten, is that right? That must have felt really good.

KEN: Oh yeah. Mother was the center of our focus as far as that, and there were times when we were much older when I would tell her that I love you very much Mother, but I just don't like what you are doing.

DR. LESSIN: Were you the youngest or were there younger kids, too?

KEN: Yes. I was the baby.

DR. LESSIN: Oh, thank you, child. So you were Kenny then?

KEN: I was Kenny Ralph Kennedy Johnston. Before I was born a funny story. The doctor used a pendulum, like a witch doctor, and the pendulum went in circles, so that meant that my mother was determined to have a little girl, and so for nine months, my name was "Patty Lou." And I had pink sheets and blankets. So when I was born, she said, "My doctor said, He's a boy.'"

A.R. was named after our father, and Jimmy was named after Mother's father, so here I am "Patty Lou." "We will name him after grandpa, Ralph Kennedy Kratz." That is how I became Ralph Kennedy Johnston. Growing up they said we can't call him Ralph, and

can't call him Kennedy, so they called me Kenny.
When I left for Military school, I changed it to Ken.

DR. LESSIN: Okay, thank you, child. Now, I would
like you to move back to the center. Try to imagine
yourself as a whole Ken again, with all your
sub-personalities, and there are more personalities
that we have not mentioned. You are aware of these
others in your body when you're making social
contacts, and there are new people present. These
others may have set up a system of rewards and
punishments that they may give you.

So, because of this, you have learned to keep feelings
and particularly your vulnerable side to yourself, then
you are ready to go back and face the public.

Imagine Ken the Professional, actually try to feel that.
And the child is there, too. At that point, what would
hurt the child's feelings? Now imagine that you're
beginning to make friends and feel good around them,
and you feel safe. You are starting to let down your
public side and just relax. You can feel the child
coming in, it is okay to be vulnerable and you can say
what is on your mind and not worry about anything.
Are there times when you actually allow yourself to
feel more emotional with some people or situations?

Now you're letting down the public side and saying this
is your girlfriend or nephew or somebody you feel safe
with. Do you feel that coming in?

KEN: When I'm comfortable, let's say, then I can let my guards down and have fun?

DR. LESSIN: Yeah, that's it. Fun. That's when the child is the one that accesses fun. Yeah, that's good. When the session is completed, we will want all to come back to form the whole person of Ken again. At that point, we will find out how much we can deal with the part of the extraterrestrial contact or the private life we don't ordinarily share when the bird comes out.

You will know that you're in charge of all of these little parts of Ken. It's only you who can assess the whole situation through which is another aspect of Ken we might call the Witness, who sees the big picture. When we are all through with this regression is when we will access the big picture, when you are feeling stronger. You need to feel centered, then we will come back to this. So, then you will be in charge of everything. Alright, you can get fully comfortable, you can lay down now.

KEN: Let me just get this pillow under my neck. Ah!

DR. LESSIN: Alright, here we go, so deep breath.

KEN: *(deep breath, slow exhale)*

CHAPTER 4

<u>E.T. GRAY BIRD</u>

CLOSE CALL

One of these events that took place in my childhood was rather peculiar. My brother Jimmy and I had grown up on the farm, with horses and shotguns for duck hunting, doing all kinds of things you would expect young boys to do on a farm. We went off one weekend as Jimmy had his drivers license.

I was only twelve at the time, we went to Muleshoe, Texas, in the "panhandle" where we met up with his good friend, and we were set up to go early in the morning out to one of the larger lakes at Muleshoe National Wildlife Refuge. We wanted to set up before sunrise and catch the ducks coming in to swim and feed. They dropped me off at a duck blind, a small haystack hideout to wait for incoming flocks, and I could then look out and see the lake.

Jimmy and his friend went around to the other side of the lake to catch the birds coming from the other end. We were using small A 4-10 shotguns, of course, we wouldn't be shooting at each other because of the size of the lake.

Once Jimmy got to the other side, a pickup truck pulled up past where we had parked, and a man got out, and for some reason, he was using a small weapon I think a 22-caliber, and began shooting down at the lake. Bullets were ricocheting across the water heading right towards the duck blind where I was.

I got a bit freaked out and started running along to where my brother was and got grazed on my left shoulder by some stray bullet. It actually pierced the leather coat I had on, and put a hole through my coat and the top of my shirt, it splayed the skin open but didn't break any bones or go deep, just a slight cut across the top of my left shoulder.

At that point, I reached a ravine that was feeding the lake with water when it rained. I jumped down in there and stayed until Jimmy and his friend came to my side of the lake and found me. After Jimmy made sure I wasn't severely hurt, we made a decision not to tell anyone, especially mom and T.C., as to not worry them or get in trouble. I still wonder to this day what the man was actually shooting at. Was he actually shooting at me to try and get rid of me, so that in the future I would be stopped from getting the truth out? Who knows? There may have been stuff around that area that the farmer followed and was shooting at something that could have been seen as a threat. Or

*is it stranger... could there have been something that
he could see that I wasn't aware of yet? Perhaps
something that landed close by.*

A STRANGE INCIDENT

[The regression continues...]

DR. LESSIN: Alright. Will you relate how it happens?

KEN: When my mother married T.C., our stepfather
was the one who used the razor strap later, all three of
us boys were together on the old farm. We use to have
some storms. And when I was little, I could get in the
window sill, put my feet up on the side, and curl up
there. We could watch the lightning and thunder there.
I always enjoyed watching the lightning. It was a really
fierce storm. It had to be October, 1948.

DR. LESSIN: And where are you?

KEN: In the window?

DR. LESSIN: Where is your house?

KEN: On the farm, the T.C. Ray farm.

DR. LESSIN: And where is that?

KEN: In Hart, Texas.

DR. LESSIN: Oh, thank you. In Hart, Texas.

KEN: My mother married T.C., and we were living in Plainview. We moved to another farm, and she married Captain Wolemdorf, a marine, US Marine Corps Captain, back from Guadal Canal. I remember us moving to this little apartment. And when we were moving things in, Jimmy and I were jumping up and down on the mattress.

And he got up on the dresser jumping off and bounces, so I gotta do the same thing, so I jump. My legs buckle, and my nose hit my knee and bloodied my nose.   My legs just weren't strong enough. We were there for just a short time. And one night my mother and Roger were yelling and screaming, and she locked the door.

And he crawls in through the window in the bathroom, falls in the bathtub. And then he leaves, and we never see him again. Later in life, I found out that he went out and committed suicide. Cause he was a Marine Captain, fought in Guadal Canal, and got a fungus in his inner ear that broke into his brain.

And the pain was so great he couldn't handle it anymore, so he put a garden hose, and hooked it up to his exhaust pipe of his car, and put it through the window, stuffed rags in the window and curled up and went to sleep. He never woke up. Then it was after that we moved to Plainview, Texas.

DR. LESSIN: But, did it affect you?

KEN: I never knew, I just knew he wasn't around anymore.   He was gone. I was only like three years old, two-and-a-half, three years old. We were in downtown Plainview with Grandma Kratz. This is where mother met T.C.   No, wait a minute. We were in the big house in Plainview and moved out to Edmonton, a little town between Plainview and Hart. Then, in Edmonton, Mother had bought a farm. Roger was trying to farm it.

The timing is hard, on that, I was only 3. A lot of fun things happened, but once he was gone, he was gone. I remember all the things on the farm and all the funny things that happened. I've told lots of people about those things.

DR. LESSIN: So, we're sitting up on the window sill watching the lightning storm.
KEN: This is T.C.Ray's farm, in Hart Texas, out in the country.

DR. LESSIN: Yep.

KEN: Closest neighbors are a mile or two away. And they called the next morning and said there was a big lightning strike or something back where I lived right across the street. I went with Jimmy and A.R. and wanted to go see it. T.C. said fine, "Go." So we put on raincoats and rubber boots, ran across the dirt road, across the barbed wire fence. A.R. was going real slow; he doesn't want to run. He was bigger and older. Jimmy and I have to compete.

I got to the fence first, and I run to the field, and I stop because there was this big flat area where all the maize has been flattened out. And right at the end of that, there was this big bird. A big whooping crane. It was as tall as I am. He turns his head, and he's looking at me. I was looking in his eyes. He was looking right at me.   He turns his head back to the front, and his big long legs, and he starts trotting, opens his wings, starts to flap his wings. He just jumps. He goes up in the air, then a couple of flaps, and just disappears.

DR. LESSIN: Okay, just keep seeing that big bird. Really get a good look, really focus hard on the big bird. While looking really close at that big bird, tell me, what do you see?

KEN: The wings were dark, but they were gray. It may be me, but the eyes are black and doesn't blink, just looks at me, then he turns his head, runs and takes off.   Jimmy and A.R. get there. And I said, "Did you see that? Did you see that?" They said, "What?" I said, "The bird. He just took off; then he's gone." They thought I was telling a joke.

DR. LESSIN: Do you think Jimmy was close enough to have been able to see it?

KEN: I don't think so. I was fast when I ran. Jimmy and A.R. didn't see it.

DR. LESSIN: Alright, put your attention back on the bird. Let's do a mental experiment. I'm going to ask you to pretend the bird is a bird suit. Now, imagine the bird suit is unzipping or falling off. Underneath the bird, see if there is anything.

KEN: Hmm. The bird is standing on the other side of the crop circle. If you unzip, you unzip, and it falls to the ground. And it runs and jumps in the air and goes, but then there is nothing on the ground, but when we unzip him, then the feathers and everything falls to the ground. It looks like a person. In fact, he runs, jumps, he's up in the air, then he's gone.
DR. LESSIN: Keep your attention on the person, seeing under the bird suit.

KEN: Somewhere, it hurts my head to focus.

DR. LESSIN: Yeah, yeah. Let that happen. Feel what is exactly happening in your head.

KEN: My forehead. It feels like all around it; my temples are tight.

DR. LESSIN: Experience that feeling. Keep that feeling, even if it gets tighter.

KEN: It makes me look, tilting to my right side.

DR. LESSIN: Stay with the feeling. Getting warm.

KEN: It's not like a headache. It's just tight on my forehead.

DR. LESSIN: Uh, huh. Okay. So, I want you to continue to feel this tightness on your forehead. Now, what I want you to allow the consciousness of the bird to give you words that you can speak, don't worry it won't take you over. Just let that being communicate with you, then tell me what the being is saying to you.

KEN: I never thought about if anything was said.
DR. LESSIN: What did it say, or not say, to you? What did that being convey to you?

KEN: It was, "Look."... "Look."

DR. LESSIN: Uh huh, "Look."

KEN: And I got cold chills just remembering it saying, "Look," and again, all my whole body is tingling. I looked, and I watched, and he turned his head, and he.... I may have seen him again. Now I'm relaxing again.

DR. LESSIN: Wow! So you think you might have seen him again?

KEN: I was… I was… just a kid.

DR. LESSIN: Yeah...?

KEN: There was a boy that you said you recognize and met... he was taller than me. Darker hair. I know we met again but I can't....

DR. LESSIN: ...if you can imagine that boy getting older...

KEN: I want to think that it was Jack but that's just a wish....Jack Lancaster is my best friend..... Military school Marine corp. We got in the dirt together and all... he's passed away.

DR. LESSIN: Go back to the ship see if you can focus on the boy.

KEN: He's taller than me.I think he had brown eyes...so it wasn't Jack...

DR. LESSIN: If you had the sense you ran into him later in life.....whoever that kid was...with Brown eyes...

KEN: It may be someone at the Academy, but I could not make that mental connection, but I know Fran that had to be her... I don't feel...

DR. LESSIN: With this connection, you don't feel the same?

KEN: No... no....

DR. LESSIN: One of those planets was Mars?

KEN: Yes I would go to Mars...

CHAPTER 5

<u>EXTRATERRESTRIAL PILOT</u>

TAKEN ABOARD AN E.T. SHIP

One of the memories that I had that was brought out during the hypnotic regression was when our extraterrestrial school teacher was taking us on a field trip in space. We went to this gigantic mothership where a craft could be parked in hangar bays. There was a dozen smaller craft that we would commonly call UFOs, or flying saucers there as well. We landed our craft inside the bay, and this short E.T. woman guided us as a group of students, walking past some of the other craft as we walked into a room.

It wasn't another hanger but more like a visitor observation deck with a giant wall of glass. We could peer out and see the stars and incoming craft floating in. Afterward, we walked into an area where there were gigantic test tube-like glass containers around three feet in diameter, and probably around six to eight feet tall. It looked like some sort of prenatal unit. Inside of each one was other species from all over the galaxy being incubated. Many looked like human baby stages in formaldehyde but were alive inside of these test tubes.

This was one of the ways of procreating the next generation of beings, to take the cells and match them up with male and female DNA so that the babies could be born inside of these test tubes. Then we walked to another area of the ship with a number of small shuttle craft. Basically, one or two person ships. We had all been trained on the planet's surface to fly these craft and had been shown how they work. I thought to myself since my father was a pilot, I was now going to become a pilot.

After this field trip, and getting to see how the craft came and went from the big mothership, we went back to the city on the surface of the planet which had a lot of greenery, streams with clean water, and fresh air. After several days, I had decided I wanted to go back home and see mother, Jimmy, and A.R. and proceeded to the docking bay where some of the smaller craft where parked.

I got into one of them and made telepathic contact with the craft's navigational systems. Low and behold, I got it to take off and flew it out of the docking bay into open space. I didn't know where the ship I were going, but my mind was made up to go back to Earth where my mother and brothers where. At that time, a much larger craft caught up with me, and put a lock, or tractor beam, on my small craft and guided me back to the mothership. It was like being in a sports race car and having a big tank pull you toward your involuntary destination.

Living through the actual experience, it isn't a surprise to me where Hollywood got some of their information about these craft. I know from that experience that there are others who have suppressed memories of similar experiences. That is just one of the things that have happened to me over the years, apparently getting groomed to fly ET craft.

THE REGRESSION CONTINUES...

DR. LESSIN: It was Mars, back to Mars, back to Mars....

KEN: Yeah, and seeing places. When I was with the space program and working to help go to the moon, it was all exciting, but I would tell people that I'm helping them go to the moon....I want to go to Mars.

DR. LESSIN: Shew... You think about Mars and think about what the dream showed you...What else do you see?

KEN: Well, ancient ruins, and I got to go fly over them. In dreams, there was always a continuation from where I was, where I went and what I got to see, and it was always fun.

DR. LESSIN: Were you with others at that time?

KEN: Just me....The odd thing is when I studied remote viewing, I'm there but I have no clothes or anything. I'm there as a spirit being or something... just no clothes on and I could fly anyplace I want to.

DR. LESSIN: I'm going to ask something strange, but imagine that you can identify with the consciousness of Mars, and it's Mars you can talk to Ken...tell him now.

KEN: Home... long time ago home. We left, we had to go. We had to go. Earth is home. Mars was home. When I go to Mars, I go and fly over places... that were some of the home places. I don't go there very often, I don't go there anymore.

DR. LESSIN: Is there an emotional feeling about that?

KEN: Only that I recognize it that it's nothing, nothing.

DR. LESSIN: Mars. I would like you to remember when we left from Mars and went to Earth. What would you like Ken to know about that?

KEN: I keep getting flashes in my eyes.

DR. LESSIN: Yes, that's gonna happen even more.

KEN: I just.... I just know we are not going back. You left home but you're coming home... Mars isn't telling me anything anymore.

DR. LESSIN: Look at the new home.

KEN: That's green trees... Mars... not like Mars was.

DR. LESSIN: Take a more extensive look around you.

KEN: No, I don't feel like anyone else is around... green trees, plants, nice things.

DR. LESSIN: Who's with you?

KEN: I don't know

DR. LESSIN: What are you wearing?

KEN: I'm wearing a jumpsuit flight suit, coveralls.

DR. LESSIN: Look at your feet.

KEN: I see my toes.

DR. LESSIN: So you didn't have shoes on?

KEN: No, it's grass, soft. There's a little clearing up front. There's a bunch of us there. I've just been out walking around. It's damp, forest, cold, I'm cold now. I don't know what they're doing now. I guess I'm just enjoying where it is I'm in the jungle.

DR. LESSIN: You're cold now?

KEN: I think my hands are cold.

DR. LESSIN: [*Dr. Lessin covers up Ken's hands while he lays on the bed*] Taking care of your hands. Take a look at the people in the clearing. Are they just sitting, visiting?

KEN: Stools... something small to sit on like a rock. I don't think this is a dream.

DR. LESSIN: I don't think so either.

KEN: I think we're resting and getting ready to do something. We are all happy. I think we're all good. It's a happy feeling, a warm feeling. I don't hear any sounds. I don't think we're talking.

DR. LESSIN: So when you're going back to work, can you tell us what that's like?

KEN: Going back to work. Hmm, going back to work makes my temples hurt.

DR. LESSIN: Are they hurting now?

KEN: Throb. Feels Like pressure pushing on my temples.

DR. LESSIN: See your hands doing some work, notice what work your doing.

KEN: I don't think it's them.

DR. LESSIN: It's OK let it shift, see what shifts.

KEN: It's kind of fun. It's almost like you can use your hands and cause things to lift and move, but you don't touch them.

DR. LESSIN: What are you moving?

KEN: I think bricks, rock blocks. I have to go see what I can push with my hands, and they move. The bigger ones we have more of a push.

DR. LESSIN: Who's pushing with you?

KEN: Just the guys. It's just what to do.

DR. LESSIN: The guys huh?

KEN: It's just what we do.

DR. LESSIN: The guys, the rocks, a good place for them to go, a good configuration?

KEN: I don't know, that's wishful thinking, but it flashed and we were pushing and stacking. Maybe making a pyramid but that cant be.

DR. LESSIN: Why can't that be?

KEN: Because that's what I want it to be.

DR. LESSIN: So why can't it be that? I understand. You're saying it can't be what you want it to be.

KEN: It's much too much to handle. From one place to another, from one happening to another. Too much happening to seem like it really happened.

DR. LESSIN: What is happening in your imagination to give us some information? Pyramids was the way many people generate electricity.

KEN: It would be just we had, what we had, and did what we had to do.

DR. LESSIN: Can you see the means by which you got there? Is there a ship?

KEN: No, I just remember we are there, and it's green and nice, and the others were there waiting. We were taking a break.

DR. LESSIN: So the others were already there, gotcha.

KEN: It was all good.

DR. LESSIN: So look around and see if there is anything else that surface at this time.

KEN: There are lots of people now. I'm up on higher
something, looking at all these people. Oh yeah.
Thousands of people. It's nice to have the people
there. It makes you feel good.

DR. LESSIN: You're getting an overview.

KEN: It's like flying, and you can fly over cities and
towns. I love flying at night. Flying at night and you
come to a town, You see the lights at night and you
feel like you're a higher being looking down. One light
is somebody's whole reason for existing. The speck of
light surrounding where they live.
In big cities, they are just scattered everywhere. That's
what you see when your flying at night. Then you find
your place, then you land. You're looking down at all
the people, it's kind of fun. I think there's a bug that got
on my cheek.

DR. LESSIN: So what do you do?

KEN: Pat him, I feel like I got cold.

DR. LESSIN: Breath deep to see if there's anything
else that's useful?

KEN: No, that I remember being there. That was
good.

DR. LESSIN: You said there was water?

KEN: In the trees, and in the plants, and in the rivers.
But it was warm. Not too hot, but a nice comfortable
moisture. I like the moisture.

DR. LESSIN: From Earth, can you look back at Mars?
What do you see? How does it feel?

KEN: Sad. Mars was not a... it was a place to be.
You can't go walking everywhere like you can Earth.
We go back to Mars.... when we go back to Mars, and
I want to go back. I don't need to go, but I would like to
go to Mars. It's funny when I say I want to go to Mars,
my right temple hurts.

DR. LESSIN: Did you remember going back to
Mars?

KEN: I didn't think I ever went back. I just dreamed of
wanting to go back.

DR. LESSIN: For a long time, you dreamed.

KEN: Yeah, and Mars, we lived on Mars. I think we
went other places too.

DR. LESSIN: Do you remember any of these other
places ?

KEN: I don't know if it's me or... I remember. I think I
remember going back to other planets, other places.
That would have to be part of me. I don't know. When
we went, and then we come back, back to Earth.

DR. LESSIN: Do you remember the moons of Mars?

KEN: When I see pictures of Phobos and Deimos. It's what we call them now. Phobos it looks, it looks more friendly than Deimos, and it's like we could have been there too.

DR. LESSIN: Could it be Phobos, do you remember?

KEN: I've seen so many pictures from our satellites that I don't know if it's in my mind or pictures I've seen. When I try to focus on Deimos, it makes my head hurt.

DR. LESSIN: See if there's something you can do to be on what you saw, on Mars moons?

KEN: Rooms, looks like caves that have been hollowed out and rooms, we have rooms that we can go into inside there. It's not all hollow but its rooms.

DR. LESSIN: Go inside of the room what is there?

KEN: There's equipment, but there's not anybody else there.

DR. LESSIN: Equipment?

KEN: Yeah, some of our stuff.

DR. LESSIN: What's it look like?

KEN: Like a control room, with our monitors and that, but not what you have now.

DR. LESSIN: What do you see on the monitor?

KEN: Nothing they are turned off. They've been shut down. We've left, we don't need to be there. There were three or four of us, and we just came to look around awhile. We left. It was like a vacation.

DR. LESSIN: I see. No particular mission... you just wanted to see.

KEN: Just went... yes it's there.

DR. LESSIN: So how do you get there and leave there?

KEN: We have our craft.

DR. LESSIN: What's it like?

KEN: A lot like the one I flew and got in trouble with.

DR. LESSIN: Hows it shaped?

KEN: It's not a round saucer. Everybody wants a flying saucer. I do have a cockpit and a place I can look out. There are different kinds. You know I can't describe the outside.

DR. LESSIN: You're seeing it from the inside looking out.

KEN: That's right. It's not a boomerang, it's not a delta wing. It's not a ball, its a thing.

DR. LESSIN: Is it making any sounds?

KEN: No. It's there waiting for the cockpit to tell it where to go.

DR. LESSIN: Can you see where you go next?

KEN: I don't know if I want to go anyplace.

DR. LESSIN: OK, notice what unfolds for you.

KEN: My head doesn't hurt when I don't go.

DR. LESSIN: There's more for you to see in dreams.

CHAPTER 6

<u>COSMIC AMBASSADOR</u>

[Editor's Note: The following passage is from Ken's Autobiography, "KEN'S MOON!   REVEALING THE "DARK MISSION" OF NASA" Ken wanted to include it because he thought it was interesting that he was with the NASA Solar System Ambassador program and also his role as an ambassador as chosen by E.T. came up in the regression.]

NEW MEXICO'S SOLAR SYSTEM AMBASSADOR FOR NASA/JPL

In the year of 2002, NASA sent out notices that they were looking for volunteers to support their new "Solar System Ambassador" program. The program was designed to present to the public through seminars, lectures, at schools, clubs, churches, and other organizations telling the story of what our nation's Space Program was accomplishing.

I presented programs to dozens of organizations enjoyed speaking to thousands of people. I still like to go out in the evenings, on occasion, and share my experiences with the Space Program. There have been opportunities to participate in media, on radio programs, several TV, and

KEN: We have to get back because there's more for
us to do. I'm having fun looking back at what we did a
long time ago, and now I've gotta go back because I'm
gonna have a job to do.

DR. LESSIN: So you go back to Mars?

KEN: No.

DR. LESSIN: No. Where do you go back to?

KEN: Earth.

DR. LESSIN: Oh so this is OK?

KEN: Go back to Earth. Back to almost now. It's like I
know what's going to happen in the near future. I'm
ready for what's gonna happen. If they do what I think?
It makes my head hurt.

DR. LESSIN: What's going to happen?

KEN: We're going too...[*pause*] ah. Our teachers, our
friends, They will come back and we will be able to
work together. So we can stop Earth from all the
hatred, and bad stuff going on. It's time, and I'm so
glad it's time.

DR. LESSIN: How are you going to stop it? That bad thing.

KEN: It's what they trained us for. They trained us to talk to the leaders. To let them know the way they've led, the way they've treated humans... That it's not good. That they have to give up and return to the good.

DR. LESSIN: Have you done everything you need to do here?

KEN: I've practiced.

DR. LESSIN: Have you tried to stop it with influential communication?

KEN: With one-on-one, or group, or on communications equipment. I've gone public to the whole world. First the face-to-face. Mostly, it's to the press people who screw things up. They think we're lying. If you tell the truth, you don't have to worry or have to go back and figure out what lie you told or who you told it too.   So we just tell the truth.

DR. LESSIN: So, when you go through the press people, they distort it and when you just talk you get to say it without it getting distorted?

KEN: Right.

DR. LESSIN: Well, that makes sense. Has anybody in authority talked to you and listened to your message?

KEN: I feel like I have, and I don't know whether it's possible that I could be in a different form, but that's what it felt like.

DR. LESSIN: Have you ever remote transported yourself to talk to an authority?

KEN: That seems more like what we have done. I keep saying we, I know there's more. Ah... No.... It's time. It's time. We have to be ready, and I don't know if the others are experiencing going back and finding out who they are? It's like we're waiting for the switch to be thrown. Maybe that's why my head hurts.

DR. LESSIN: What's this switch?

KEN: It just opens up our mind then we know what we have to say, where we're at and what's going on. What's past and what's future.

It's all there but it's like you're waiting to access things... it hurts the head.

DR. LESSIN: How can you get people whose main concern is National Security to hear your message?

KEN: [*Breathing... Sigh...*] We will have to arrange meetings to where they have the chance to meet. Who we were before, those that were here before. So this is why we are trying to become an ambassador. I guess that's why they took us to so many places.

DR. LESSIN: Imagine the time is right for the shift, for the switch. What do you fantasize that might be like?

KEN: Lots of disbelief... a little panic. A little listening to understand that it's all for good.

DR. LESSIN: How do your teachers say to deal with those who perpetrated evil?

KEN: It's not my job. It's not my job to take care of them; they are going to hurt themselves.   My job is to talk to those that have open minds that want to learn, and they are willing to learn.

DR. LESSIN: If you could talk to one person face-to-face to tell of your experiences and what you want to teach? Who would you choose?

KEN: Donald Trump right now.

Dr. Lessin: A person that's likely to be president of the United States.

KEN: I think so, yeah. He might just...

DR. LESSIN: He knows something.

KEN: I didn't know that. Ones I wouldn't talk too, they have closed minds, they think they have all the control in the world......Big Surprise.

DR. LESSIN: So, you do see Trump, President Trump... what do you say?

KEN: Mr. President, I'd like for you to meet Enki. That would be more than Donald Trump could handle. I think that would be an opening. I had forgotten how big they were.

DR. LESSIN: ... and now you're remembering.

KEN: Oh... scary. I always wondered growing up what it would be like talking face to face with an EBE. Now I think it might be a little scary. If they're that big...

I never thought of them as big. I always thought of myself looking at them eye-to-eye.

DR. LESSIN: We might come up to the top of his knees from the old drawings.

KEN: Yeah, maybe we will be like little babies looking up at our parents, and look at them with awe... and they just look at us with love. Then it's a good feeling.

DR. LESSIN: So, if you could, just for the moment, identify with Enki... as you perceive with Enki.

KEN: Well, I had an adequate flash of a biblical term but it's not what I ... I don't know?

DR. LESSIN: What's the term?

KEN: "Good job, my son." No... ah... [*sigh*]... I don't know if he would even talk to me. I don't know whether he'd just nod, and maybe a nod's all I need.

DR. LESSIN: Yes, you're doing the right thing.

KEN: That's what we need to do.

DR. LESSIN: Now just take in the presence of Enki for a bit. See what it tells you.

KEN: There are others, not just Enki. There are others. I don't know if they were the other people on the big ship we saw, with the babies in the bottles, but there were others there too. It's just not the ones we call the Annunaki. It's a gathering of people that are willing to listen.

CHAPTER 7

<u>GUIDED BY FATHER'S HAND</u>

WHAT HAPPENED TO MY DAD

Around 1942, the year after Pearl Harbor, my father was a Captain in the Army Air Corps that would later become the Air Force. My father, Captain Abraham Russel Johnston, was in training to become one of the bomber pilots that would have gone to Europe on air raids over Germany. His best friend was still a flight instructor for the small fighter planes and there was a hurricane coming into the Gulf. Hurricanes have always been a key factor in my family's life.

I was born on October 2nd, 1942. A family story is that I "met" the future President of the United States, Dwight D. Eisenhower who was a Colonel at the time. Eisenhower and his wife Mamie were close friends with my father and mother.

Colonel Eisenhower was the base commander at Ft. Sam Houston, in San Antonio, Texas. They would get together with my parents to play bridge on the weekends when things were settled down and quieter.

I was a baby then and Dwight volunteered to hold me for a minute while my mom went to the kitchen to get some coffee and snacks for everyone. At any rate, I "wet" on the future president and he held me straight out with his arms, looked at my mother and said "Here take him. I think he's sprung a leak." I told this story to his great-granddaughter, Laura Eisenhower, and she was delighted to hear a personal incident about him.

The war was going on and we had already been pulled into the war after the attack on Pearl Harbor by the Japanese. My dad's best friend, who was still a fighter pilot instructor, contacted dad when a hurricane hit in the Corpus Christi area.

The friend asked if my dad if he could fly some student pilots back north to get them safely out of the hurricane zone. My dad agreed and said, "Sure."

They took a DC3 "Gooney Bird," flew north above Kansas, and picked up the eleven students, leaving their planes behind. On their way flying back, toward a mountain with a cliff wall called Council Bluffs, something happened with the airplane, the engine failed on them, they were unable to clear the mountain and they crashed into that mountains, killing all thirteen pilots along with my father.

This left me and my brothers without a father. I was only two-and-a-half months old when I lost my dad in that plane crash.

moment, chills hit me that, "Yes," my father knew who I was and that I existed. When I was first learning to fly there were times when I could feel his gloved hands over mine, guiding me as I would fly the airplane. Just that one event with the pictures proved to me that my dad knew who I was.

CONTIUING THE REGRESSION...

KEN: I feel like I'm going to get to see my dad again.

Dr. Lessin: he's not too far...

KEN: When I did my first solo flight, Captain Schultz got out of the plane and said, "Take it around make three "touch and goes," and come in for a full landing." I took off and made my first approach and go around, and I'm lined up and coming down. I'm flying with a control stick, not a yoke, just like a regular fighter, and I feel these warm hands around my hands helping me control the airplane down... *(getting choked up)* to make a "touch and goes" to make full power and I take off again and he ... I feel my dad... his hands...holding my hands... and in my life, there have been other times.

I remember the time when my brother rolled the car several times and we were grabbed and held tight... the car rolled and we were set down on the ceiling of the car safe and sound, and the time when the car came around and forced me off the road, and the car rolled two-and-a-half times, and the roof caved in and I felt like I was being held sitting in this seat and the ceiling and windows were smashed down, and I rolled off to the side, so I didn't get hurt.

He has been with me all through my life keeping me safe. I have talked to my dad many times, and I know that he's answered, and I know that he's... I just want him to be proud of the good that I've done.

DR. LESSIN: How would he respond to that can you sense that?

KEN: It's just a smile

DR. LESSIN: *(joyous laugh)* You did good son...

KEN: Yeah, you did good, and my brother Jimmy and my brother A R.... he couldn't handle the stress, and now I've grown older than him. I've now grown older than my mother was. I've outgrown them all. I truly think that I can live to 180 at least.

Just whatever my goals and objectives are and whatever they need me for I will live long enough to do that, or I'll do whatever I'm supposed to do.... *(sniffle. ... sigh...)* That has been a trip. A great trip and I'm still loving every moment of it and I want to go more.

DR. LESSIN: Before we leave your parents, there is something you want to say to your father and mother what would you say to each of them?

KEN: Other than, "I have loved you and I miss you and see you soon. When you're ready to come back." I don't think I will be crossing over for a long time, but they'll be there, and... *(with a sincere tone)*... thanks for the help. Thanks for the help. That's good. That's good they've all helped.

DR. LESSIN: Do you have anything to say to the fella that strapped you, your stepdad?

KEN: Yes...and it took until Karen had me write my autobiography and I had to go back and relive these experiences.

CHAPTER 8

<u>NASA'S PROTECTIVE LAYERS</u>

"TRUTH'S PROTECTIVE LAYERS"

[Editor's Note: The phrase, "Truth's Protective Layers" was uttered by Neil Armstrong, first man to step on the moon from the Apollo missions. Ken's testimony as a whistleblower has been featured in many documentaries, videos, mainstream TV programs, and on countless radio programs.

Ken's story, along with a large body of work from anomalists and researchers that find many aspects of our NASA space program that are confusing and puzzling. The quote by Armstrong is an odd one, considering the hero status that he has attained.

"Today we have with us a group of students, among America's best. To you, we say we have only completed a beginning. We leave you much that is undone. There are great ideas undiscovered, breakthroughs available to those who can remove one of truth's protective layers. There are places to go beyond belief. Those challenges are yours–in many fields, not the least of which is space, because there lies human destiny."

*The phrase "There are places to go beyond belief,"
is intriguing. The questions that Ken gets all the time
when he talks to people:*

"Did we go to the moon?"

"Did we have help going to the moon?"

*"Are they hiding the evidence of what
the astronauts found there on the moon?"*

*The public, who footed the bill for the Apollo missions,
is not going to be answered, apparently, until we
penetrate NASA's "protective layers."*

*Ken's experience has become part of the quest that so
many are on these days to find out the truth... under
those layers. ~ K.C.P., Editor]*

STORY OF THE APOLLO 14 FILM

DR. LESSIN: Imagine you're on a building on the
73rd floor. there is an ELEVATOR that your facing. It
says 73, and your going to get in the elevator, and
your hand goes to a button on the wall to how old you
were at the critical incident that happened that will help
you understand most of what you wish to explore.

Go into the elevator and push a button to correspond
to how old you were. Say what floor-button you push.

KEN: Seven

DR. LESSIN: So you went to the seventh floor.
Relive the thoughts, emotions, smells, sights of this
experience. Say what is happening in the present
tense, what is happening now in this critical incident.

KEN: *(clears throat)* I have to go from a... the data
receiving lab to the photo department in the other
building and check out a roll of 16mm film that Dr.
Page wanted me to check out, so that I could set it up
and show it to some of the other scientists as well.

It's nice out. The sun is shining and I don't remember
the number of the film, and I really want to know the
number of the film, but I got the right film, and took it
over to set it up and show it. and ah, the building is
next to the Mission Control building at the Johnson
Space Center, and... at the main conference room
they had a 16mm projector waiting for me.

I opened the top of the canister and put in the end on
the top reel, threaded it through the machine, and got
it all set up for Dr. Page and six other scientists. We
turned the lights off and I start the projector so we
could watch what was being filmed during the Apollo
14 flight on the back side of the moon, and it was just
like the pictures of craters and everything, and we're
coming around and approaching a crater, I knew it was
called Tsiolkovsky, a very big crater, 125 kilometers
wide.

In the shadow part, in the shade, there was a cluster of lights, like balloons or like domes... about five of them, all clustered together. Dr. Page had me stop the camera and then back the reel up, and come forward again. Zoom in close, look at it, back up again... and Dr. Page turns around looking at the other scientists and said, "What do you think of that guys?" They all had a good laugh.

Here I am, excited because I was looking at domes, and something unnatural on the moon, an alien base or something, and I'm really excited because he tells me I can finish the showing. And I looked forward to showing it tomorrow, or the next day. Take it to someone else so that they get a chance to see it. I remember those domes just as clear as day.

Checking it back into the photo lab. And the next day I'm showing it to everyone else, and we're coming up on the crater again with my brother A.R. in the projection booth with me, and in the shadow area, THIS TIME THERE IS NOTHING THERE!!!

A.R. asked me what was I trying to show him, and he said, "I thought there was an alien base there or something?" But it was gone. I re-checked it all and fixed the film. I confirmed that it wasn't, Brother Johnston... or spliced and finished, showing it for everybody. They were happy to see all the craters and the back side of the moon. So here I am, thinking of what I saw the previous day.

DR. LESSIN: So how does it make you feel emotionally?

KEN: I knew right away that somebody had done something to remove them. So when I checked them back in to the photo lab, and left the building, I ran into Dr. Page and asked him, "What happened to the domes in the crater we saw yesterday?" He winked and said, "There was nothing there."

There was so much going on... we were so busy all of the time, We couldn't go back and try to look at the canisters. I never got a chance to. I know when I checked out the film, that I had to write down in the log what the can number was that I had to check out. I really want to know the number to that film.

DR. LESSIN: Take a look at it again.

KEN: On the canister of the film, I see a white label card, Apollo 14 written on the top row, for some reason I see a "6."

DR. LESSIN: Is there something in front of the "6?"

KEN: A "4" and a "3."

DR. LESSIN: Are they in the front or the back?

KEN: They are up to the 6... there should be an "AS14," but I cant see it.

DR. LESSIN: So we have "6," "4," "3," and it should be "AS14."

KEN: They had to identify all the reels with each mission. Maybe they are smaller numbers and small letters, but it's on the canister. I wrote it down when I checked it out. I would say it is in the logbook.

DR. LESSIN: Yes, take a look at the log book.

KEN: OK, The logbooks were on the counter, and I don't recall a person behind this... and I'm gonna have to check this out. I don't remember if I went in and got it or if someone brought the canister to me.

DR. LESSIN: Who writes in the logbook?

KEN: I wrote it down in there, so it has my name, the reel numbers, the date, and time. It was like a sheet of paper on a clipboard.
DR. LESSIN: What's the date?

KEN: I don't see the date.

DR. LESSIN: OK

KEN: "October 14" comes to mind but that doesn't mean anything.

DR. LESSIN: So now you're aware that you've been "winked" into a secret that people on the base aren't getting. They were denied the view you had.

KEN: Well, it was so disappointing that I knew that we'd seen evidence of extraterrestrial life on the back side of the moon. Now they've hidden it, and now I don't have time, I can't go back and get it, and so it becomes a question of whether people believe me or not.

I didn't tell anybody for a long time. It was a friend that later was in charge of the public relations film. He was a member of the World Wide Church, and I told him. He believed me, but he had to keep things hidden, too.

It was so disappointing. I was so excited about it, I wanted to show everybody what we had seen, and then I couldn't do that anymore.

So life moves on, and kids, problems, and things. Marriage changing, divorce, all kinds of things. I retired, and now I had time to think about those things. I think that log has to be in a photocopy somewhere.

DR. LESSIN: Yeah. Take another look at the log, and see if you can see more details.

KEN: Just your typical Xerox copy of a page, just the date, the name and the item you want, and when you checked it out, you checked it back in.

DR. LESSIN: See your hand with a pen, a pencil.

See what that looks like. What did you write?

KEN: On the date, I remember a "9..." "9-24-71."
Then print my name... then the item that I want.

DR. LESSIN: "6..."... "4..."... "3."

KEN: I put "AS14," and it would have to be "Apollo
Reel 14..." ... "AS14-88-8643," ... "91" ... maybe I
wrote too small? I don't know.

CHAPTER 9

<u>I SEE FRAN</u>

[Editor's note: An interesting scene in the regression is where Ken has a "future memory" of seeing many people from his life on a ship in an abduction scenario. Other experiencers have reported having had similar memories. ~ KCP]

KEN: We moved to Norman Oklahoma. T.C. Ray was with us, and he doesn't like the big city. Norman was a big town, and we had a big three-story apartment building for students, and we made the decision to move back to Texas.

When I was in Norman, I had dreams and times when I think about the big bird. We went back to Hart Texas, The families all got together to build a house for us a block away from where the school is where we took Kindergarten all the way through 12th grade.

At night there was a lot of noise, and everybody wanted to go outside and see what was going on. Between our house the railroad track and grain elevators, with all the empty fields, and so we all went outside, and there were people gathered around looking at this thing that landed in this field.

Something else happens later on this site and I don't want to forget, about the ants in this field, but right now this thing is here this ship. There were shimmering

lights all around, and everybody's looking at it, and no one seems to be scared.

The lights come on and a door opens and a ramp comes down, and this tall blond guy walks out, everyone else starts panicking and running. He points to me and signals for me to come to him, and I just walked right over to it, I'm not afraid. I walked up the ramp and went inside of the craft and there were other people there, and their all applauding, They said to come in.

DR. LESSIN: The people are inside?

KEN: Yes. It's like where the ramp come up inside, and there, some of them leaning over and coming down, they are saying come in. The next thing I remember, I'm in Training. Wherever their home is, and they were willing to teach me, well they taught me how to fly the spacecraft. They went on to teach me how to teach people on Earth to be friendly.

DR. LESSIN: With that, how do you fly the craft? Did they show you?

KEN: Ah... It's... You sit in an area not quite like an airplane it's, instruments and things that react to what you think. You're not pushing buttons or moving controls and things; it's whatever you think. That's what the ship does. I even tried to take one of the small ones and go back to Earth, and they caught me and told me not to do that anymore.

DR. LESSIN: You actually flew?

KEN: Yeah, I was flying a little one.

DR. LESSIN: How did they catch you, What do you mean?

KEN: The bigger ship just kind of caught the little craft and brought me back inside the bay of the bigger ship, but it was fun.

DR. LESSIN: Who's the "they," tell me about the "they?"

KEN: Like the ones I met when I first came on board. Tall, Blond, and we were taken to be with the kids.

DR. LESSIN: There were other kids?

KEN: Yah! We were all there to be trained. We were on a trip to another big ship and we were being herded around by a different type of person, like a teacher, and we all just follow her. We went to a laboratory

where they looked like babies in bottles. They said
these are growing.

DR. LESSIN: You said it was a different kind of
person?

KEN: This person was smaller, much smaller. I think
it was a woman, but nice, really nice, Taking us around
and showing us different things. I see a bronze kind of
color. Bronze colored but nice.

DR. LESSIN: She's bronze-colored?

KEN: Yes, but not real dark. Just a light shade of
bronze. Something happens and they have to get us
to go back. I have these dreams almost like I never left.
I have dreams of going to different planets, particularly
Mars.

In this dream of Mars, I'm standing at the edge of this
big canyon and it's like I just lean forward and lift my
arms and I'm flying, I go down and I'm going across
land and coming up on old ruins ancient ruins. You can
tell that it was somebody's. When I'm older, I see ruins
in the desert, and Saudi Arabia, and ancient ruins a lot
like what I saw on Mars.

DR. LESSIN: Well, what does it look like?

KEN: Like looking down on Hiroshima and Nagasaki,
explosions, but I think they are just so old that they
crumbled.

DR. LESSIN: When you say crumbled you mean?

KEN: Yeah, these dreams I keep having as I grow older, I get fewer dreams, and then I'm so busy with Military and getting married and having kids, and later on further in life I start having the dreams again. I start practicing on being able to meditate and am able to remote view and how to communicate with my mind and I'm getting good at it.

Then all the sudden it's like the switch is thrown and I have the great ringing in my head and my ears. Then I can't focus or communicate with them anymore and I don't know why. I guess I bothered everybody... I like to ask questions.

DR. LESSIN: Let's go back to when you were with this light bronze teacher. See if you can recall a little bit more. What did you ask her?

KEN: I asked about the babies, and she said that they are growing and that they are almost ready to be born. I remember seeing the babies in the bottles; they were big bottles, not small.

Years later in the Houston Museum, they had bottles of fetuses at different stages, but these were not that way. These were full-sized babies with umbilical cord. They were alive and moving inside this fluid, they were in this, not bottles but more like tubes and the teacher thought to think we saw some other kids. They were other kids that didn't quite look like us.

DR. LESSIN: What did they look like?

KEN: They were small, smaller than us. They seemed to be happy like we were happy.

DR. LESSIN: Where they part of the...

KEN: I think they were a different group, as there were several groups, We were taken for experiments.

DR. LESSIN: Do you remember details of a particular group? They were in your group.

KEN: Yes, there was one guy, I know I met him before but I can't remember where, but I know I met him again on Earth.

DR. LESSIN: They were in your group up there?

KEN: Yes. When I was back to where I was on Earth, I know that I've run into them and we looked at each other like we knew each other. It's just a strange feeling you get, but how could you know them if you hadn't met them? It's just strange.

DR. LESSIN: Do you remember their names?

KEN: I don't think we used names, we were just us.

DR. LESSIN: So you were in a group of these people?

KEN: That's correct. I was just thinking because of who I met much later here in life, that I know who has had experience with ET's and the fact that we instantaneously took to each other, When I met Fran, and a month and a half later we married.

DR. LESSIN: Oh my gosh.

KEN: We've been married for 33 years this year.

DR. LESSIN: So what is your wife's name?

KEN: I am wondering if she isn't the girl that was there, I had never thought of that.

DR. LESSIN: So what is your wife's name?

KEN: Fran.

DR. LESSIN: Could she have been the girl that was on the ship with you?...

KEN: That would be cool.

DR. LESSIN: Take a really good look at the way the girl, the way she really looks.

KEN: I've got the tingling again... We were kids, we were little kids...well, older than when we first met around 12-13. ... Wow... I think that's her....

DR. LESSIN: Look into her eyes.

KEN: Shaking with tears, Wow.... I can't wait to tell
her...

DR. LESSIN: what do you want to say to Fran?
KEN: (Choked up....) good to see you again.....I....
Fran and I ...I can't wait to tell her that I think I know
where we met....that was amazing.

KEN: 7 is a sacred number to me. And even
though..... I just like the number 7.

DR. LESSIN: Just go to the 7th floor go where you're
seven years old. Tell me what you're doing?

KEN: I can take the elevator and go down to the 7th
floor, and the door can open and I can walk in. I'm
going into a room. Where everybody knows me and
we know each other, It's like a gathering room. I get
that cold feeling that chill again.... I.. I didn't know that
wow...It's like going in for a family reunion. We're all
getting together again. I like that.

DR. LESSIN: Who's there?

KEN: The ones who were on the ship, the students.

DR. LESSIN: They're all there, wow.

KEN: I.. I... Wow. *(sigh... exhale)*

DR. LESSIN: Do you see Fran there?

KEN: I haven't looked around. *(chuckles)* There are people I didn't know were there. There are people there that thought I was crazy, too. Hey, they're there. I'm looking for Fran. Yeah, there she is, on the other side. *(laughing)* She's there! *(sniffing, chuckle)* She's there! Oh! *(laugh)* It's overwhelming! *(teary voice)* To see everybody together...

DR. LESSIN: Yes, feeling it...

KEN: And ... we can all be together again. *(sniffle, sigh)* We can come up and settle the truth... and we don't have to worry about... keeping it a secret for our integrity, for our... so that people can know that what we've been taught is real. That these people are the ones, who have been there and have done it, too.... Oh... *(sniffle... sigh)* I've never opened the door before. Fran's gonna be surprised when I get home.

DR. LESSIN: Sit with the room and express what's happening.

KEN: I think we're all happy, we are applauding each other. Every time the door opens and another one comes in; we are all applauding saying, "Hi guys were here! *(sniffles)*

DR. LESSIN: Wow!

KEN: I feel cold and nervous though. It's like this is just too much. *(big exhale)*

DR. LESSIN: Whatever you feel is appropriate.

KEN: I don't know whether we've done it before, or were doing it now, but it's gonna happen again. The pain in the head doesn't hurt anymore. The tightness in my forehead is like a fuzzy warmth. It feels better.

DR. LESSIN: If you can feel the ambiance of this whole group, the collective feeling...

KEN: It's like we all know each other, and we've all been doing our part, and were all part of the same goal and objective, and that is to make things right. To tell the truth, and to re-educate. We are all teachers. Even though we just get it started. The work has just begun, and it's going to be GOOD. Those that are afraid, "Don't be afraid." It's all good. (sniffles)

DR. LESSIN: In that room, is there someone who you would particularly like to address now?

KEN: (long pause) Yeah, our teacher. The bronze being...

DR. LESSIN: What do you say to her?

KEN: It's more what she said, or "thought" to us. She says, "You did Good. *(choke up)* That you guys have, "done good." So... ah... I've never been there before.

(exhale) It's kind of like having a mother compliment you and tell you that you've done something good. So that's good. *(big sniffle... sigh relieved)* oh wow... that's something.

DR. LESSIN: Just breath out...

KEN: I know they all thought the same thing. It's not just me...We've been pulled together as a team, and I don't know how... I feel tears down my face. I've been put together with the team, and I can go back to Hoagland and the others that I've come in contact with, and even debunkers are making a positive influence because they are telling everyone, "Don't look at this," and of course, that is exactly what people will do, Look.

We're looking at it that way, so it's his problem, not mine. (laugh) With Karen, Donna, and Bret and others that are joining the team are all a part to help us as this unfolds. The team grows, and I am just so blessed to be a part of it.

DR. LESSIN: Just imagine if you would, get back on the elevator, press the 73rd button, coming up toward the top, floor 69, 68, getting closer... 69... 70 almost to the top.... 72... 73, and you wake up.

KEN: Oh, waking up.....oh wow... (stretching, breathing)

DR. LESSIN: When you're ready, reflect on it.

KEN: I'm glad I know how to breathe.

DR. LESSIN: In through the nose, out through the mouth.

KEN: I've gone places I haven't been in a long time.

DR. LESSIN: You can sit up now......

KEN: Wow, am I dizzy.

DR. LESSIN: Change your orientation.

KEN: I'm shaky. There were times when I thought I was in control and other times when I knew I wasn't.

DR. LESSIN: You can feel that there is this part of you that has recall.

KEN: Yes.

DR. LESSIN: You can decide how much and when.

KEN: I can take myself back when I want to right?

DR. LESSIN: You don't have to slavishly say everything.

KEN: There are so many out there that make contact, that I will find or will find me. Like Fran. that was emotional. God, that was great.

DR. LESSIN: You've probably been together many lifetimes.

KEN: I think so...

[END OF REGRESSION SESSION]

After the regression, when I was brought back to the here and now, I woke up feeling like I was cold, shivering, nervous... had been crying. I felt flush.

I was becoming aware of all these things that have happened to me in the past, and yet just kind of in shock, realizing that I hadn't been under hypnosis for fifteen or twenty minutes like I thought, but more than two hours went by.

Dr. Lessin had pointed out that as time goes by, after this experience, that I would start remembering a lot more, in my present state of consciousness, of all these events that took place in my life that made me who I am today.

This experience is giving me more and more understanding of why I had been chosen to do what I am here to do; bringing the truth forward, so that everyone can see what's really going on. I realized that there is a lot more going on in this universe than most people think.

I just recently came to the realization that so much of what we think and imagine is true, isn't in our consensus reality. So much of what the E.T.'s had plans for people like me, who have experienced these things first hand, are here to be part of FULL AND TOTAL DISCLOSURE, putting the pieces of the puzzle together, one experience at a time.

I realized that I do have a duty and that all these things that I have experienced in my life have prepared me to be able to handle those that are going to debunk anything that I've ever said. I have the documents and evidence to prove in any normal court that everything that I've said here is the truth. Experiencers like me are here to prepare us, as a species, to ready to become a cognizant, intelligent, peaceful space-faring species in the Universe. That is my duty and that is my job, and why I was to be put in this position at this time.

CHAPTER 10

FRAN'S E.T. ENCOUNTERS

By Frances "Fran" Helen Johnston,

I was born on December 3, 1949, and I was raised in British Columbia Canada for the most part. I was named Frances Helen (after my grandmother) Marlene Marshall, and I was born in Vancouver, BC. But, spent most of my first 11 years on the Sechelt Peninsula in Edmont, British Columbia with my mother, father, and three brothers in Edmont, BC. My brothers were Billie, Donnie and later Calvin.

My father was a logger and fisherman and was gone for a good portion of the time, so we were raised by my mother. We lived approximately a mile from the village and had to walk to school through the forest. Our closest neighbors were about 1/2 a mile away. Living on the ocean, we had access to food at any time. My mother canned just about everything she could get for us. I have a lot of good memories of the little village in which we lived.

When I was 7, I moved with my grandparents to Ottawa, Ontario to keep my grandmother company while my grandfather, Calvin Reiz, who was in the Royal Canadian Air Force, was off doing maneuvers. After a year and a half, we moved back to British Columbia and back to Edmont. It was quite a culture shock going from a large city back to a little fishing village.

In September of 1959, my father William James Marshall (found out in my 60s that this wasn't his actual name, more on that later), brothers Billy and Donnie drowned in a boating accident, and everything changed that day.

I still remember a lot of what happened that day when we were alerted by our neighbors and when the police boat showed up informing my mother that they couldn't find their bodies.

We had a funeral for them with an empty casket. I remember crying because I knew what was going on and my mother finally realized that I was traumatized by the loss as well. This whole thing was hard on my mother as she was also pregnant with my youngest brother Robert. My mother had to wait the obligatory four years to announce my father's death.

We moved to Vancouver, BC to live with my grandparents, and wait for my youngest brother Robert to be born. It was difficult for my mother is now a single parent, with two kids and one on the way but we survived.

After a couple of years, we moved to Surrey with my grandparents after they bought their first home. My grandparents helped raise the 3 of us, and it was financially a big help for my mother. About a year later, my mother won a substantial sum from an Irish Sweepstakes race, and she bought a house right across the street.

I still remember waking up one early morning, looking out the back window of our house and seeing what looked like a flotilla of flying saucers. I never told anyone at that time because they would have considered me out of my mind.

A couple of years later, she married a man, and he became my first stepfather who I had to forgive to forget. I despised this man with a passion. Neither of us liked each other, probably because I figured out what he was up to, wanting my mother's assets.

My mother was married to him for approximately 18 months before we finally left in the middle of the night. I remember taking my babysitting money and helping to arrange for the Greyhound bus to pick us up on a frigid night in December on the side of the road. She did get a divorce from him shortly afterward. We moved back to our old house in Surrey. Luckily my mother hadn't listened to my ex-stepfather and didn't sell it like he wanted her to do.

One evening, I was having a terrible time missing my father and two brothers, I laid there crying desperately to be taken away from the bad situation with my mother and where we were at the time. She was working two jobs, partying with my uncles and ignoring my two brothers and myself. I remember laying there and then saw three shrouded figures standing beside my bed.

They didn't scare me, and I was asked what was wrong. I told them that I was sure my father hadn't died, and he was going to come back and get me. They indicated to me that they had passed and that everything was going to be good from then on, just have faith. Things did seem to get better after that.

In 1971, I married my first husband, and I had two beautiful girls. He had a very volatile personality, but I didn't realize it until after we married. We divorced after seven years but only because it took me three years to find him. Canadian divorce laws were different.

In 1973, my mother married my second stepfather, an American Citizen, Dale Boline and they lived happily in Canada for a few years. However, he was seriously injured in a semi truck accident and had to have one of his legs amputated below the knee. There aren't a lot of job opportunities for amputees, so they moved to Marysville, Washington, USA, and he got a job with the Boeing company. In 1977, he suggested that I get my green card and move to the US where there were more job opportunities, and so the process began to get cards for my daughters and myself.

So I began the process to obtain immigrant status for my daughters and me in the US. After going through the legal process of fingerprints, medicals, TB tests and background checks for me and my two daughters, three and five at the time. In 1980, we made the giant leap to move from Vancouver, British Columbia to Marysville Washington.

We took the clothes on our backs and whatever else we could cram into a 1975 Honda and prayed for a good outcome. But on a side note, I also had a woman read my tea leaves, and she told me almost to the exact month that I would leap to my next life.

I immediately found a job at a Mexican fast food restaurant where I worked for two months. Then an advertisement showed up in the newspaper for a large aerospace company in Seattle who was hiring several hundred people. There, of course, is only one significant aerospace company in Seattle so I went and applied at the contracting company as they were hiring temps instead of full-time employees. The first appointment I had was for a basic interview and the second was for a typing test which was on a Thursday.

During the second interview, HR from Boeing called and said they needed four clerks on Monday. She looked at me and asked if I wanted the job. I said yes, and that was the start of my 15-year career at Boeing. My mother had a fit, telling me that I shouldn't give up a job with the fast food place because the position at Boeing might end at any time.

I started with Boeing as a temporary employee in July 1980 and was hired on as a full-time employee in August of 1980. What a relief that was because Boeing had decided not to hire any more temp employees after August of that year.

My boss, Patricia Dennis, was not easy to work for, but she was fair. Every opportunity that popped up where I could learn new skills I jumped in with both feet which is where I had my start with computers. Everyone else in our area didn't want to touch them, but the opportunity gave me a jump start moving forward with opportunities. I took several classes when offered. My daughters and I lived with my parents for a while until I was able to get on feet. They purchased two houses in Marysville, and I rented one of them which helped me immensely. My mother babysat for me which was another Godsend.

In 1981, I joined Parents Without Partners (PWP) and met several wonderful people and some that were not so wonderful, but I found a way to socialize at least. My daughters and I had several fun outings with people who only wanted to be with others. We would go dancing at specific locations and just enjoy the company.

The house that I rented from my mother was a two story with a full basement. The girls and I lived upstairs in the three bedroom part because we didn't need the full basement. One night my daughter Deanna who was six at the time, told my mother that she had seen an alien outside her bedroom window on the second floor. My mother, who didn't believe in aliens, told her that she was dreaming, then she told her that it was near Halloween and her uncles had put on a mask to scare her.

The only way that they could have scared her was to get on a ladder and peek in the window near midnight. I learned about the alien incident later on, but my daughter refuses to discuss the episode even to this day. For a long time, when I tried to get her to talk about it, she would get into a fetal position and hide. She has never discussed what the alien looked like or anything like that to this day and she is 43.

So I continued my job at Boeing, meeting people at PWP and socializing. Several of the guys would say things like, do you want to see my trains, my etchings. Get real! No! I decided to become the public relations VP, and it seemed that anyone who had enough confidence to do that sort of job. In August of 1984, I went to a regular meeting where we danced, had munchies and drank if we so chose to. A friend of mine, Jennie, told me that she found someone that she wanted me to meet. My thoughts were, here we go again!

So I danced with Ken Johnston. He was well dressed, danced well and smelled good. He said to me "I bet you're wondering why a guy who was married for 17 years is doing here?" My thoughts were, No, this is PWP, I would expect a divorcee to be here. However, there was a Canadian woman there who had set her sights on him as well. After being on my own for eight years, I could support myself and my two daughters. I wasn't looking for a relationship; I had enough of men.

That weekend was also a big PWP conference where people from Canada and the US came for fun and learning. We met up at another dance that weekend, and we ended up dancing just about all night together. The Canadian woman and another one were after Ken pretty ambitiously. Again, I was completely independent, so I just went my way.

The next day, we had several meetings that Ken attended with one of the other women. I smiled and talked to Ken, found out he worked at Boeing as well. I asked him what his mail address was at Boeing. I noticed that he was eating a Snickers bar which he said was his favorite. On the next workday, I sent a Snickers bar to his mail address in Boeing with my phone number. And so it began, the whirlwind romance. However, Ken was also testing the waters with three other women.

My daughters finally met him after two weeks. He was wearing a complete Native American outfit, headdress and all, mopping my floor. My girls thought that I had lost my mind.

We started living together after about three weeks. One of the days, Ken told me he had made a date a month before with one of the ladies to take her to an October-Fest dance. While he was out with this woman, I did his laundry. When he came home that night and informed me that I had folded his socks wrong, that about ended everything right then and there. He quickly realized that he made a huge mistake with that statement.

A week later he had been given orders to go to Santa Maria to work at Vandenberg Air Force base. He told me that I didn't want to be married to a civilian astronaut, but I did.

On October 31st, he proposed to me in front of a woman who thought he was going to propose to her. Ken didn't realize that she was head over heels in love with him. He asked me if I would marry him and I said, I would have to think about it for three days and said "Yes" right then and there.

We went to the Halloween party and had a great time. I was dressed as a pirate, he was dressed as a Native American chief, and the woman who thought he was going to propose to was dressed as a Native American woman.

His military orders came quickly after, so we had to make plans quickly. In 3 days, we sent out invitations, found a minister, set up the wedding ceremony, bought a cake, and were told by everyone who attended that, "it wouldn't work." So on November 5, 1984, we were married.

My girls and friends were there. My daughters got into the champagne and cake, making them quite ill so we went home instead of going out to dinner as planned. We can laugh at that now.

While we were in Orcutt, California, which is a suburb of Santa Maria, we were outside one evening and saw an object moving across the sky. It had eight red lights, none of them flashing, no sound, and couldn't see what this object was. Several people witnessed it. It has haunted me for years.

AFTERWORD

By Dr. Sasha Lessin

HYPNOSIS EXPANDS ALIEN CONTACT MEMORIES: The Regression of Ken Johnston Sr. by Dr. Sasha Lessin. (edited for length for inclusion in this book)

I present in this chapter the method I used in my now-famous hypnosis session with Ken Johnston Sr. This method is for you to try on your own, with a partner or in an experiencer group.

ACCESS EXTRATERRESTRIALS THOUGH YOUR CENTER

If you're an extraterrestrial or inter-dimensional Contactor, you may have suppressed an inner voice that agreed to your contacts. Perhaps you agreed and forgot you did. Maybe you remember E.T.s invaded you, and think they did so against your will.

But a protective part of you – a primary sub-self – labeled the contact to which you agreed as "involuntary." Your primary self may have hidden from your awareness that you said "yes" to paranormal, or extraterrestrial contact. Sometimes, after extensive therapy and maturity, you realize a part of you – a suppressed sub-personality, alter, part, or repressed inner voice – did say "yes' to contact.

Your social or primary sub-selves can push your Inner Contactor, a voice inside your head, from your conscious awareness to shield you from conventional people who'd shame, punish, or even lock you away for recalling and speaking of your ET or other paranormal experiences.

But it can be safe now to let yourself to experience part of you that wants you to remember your experiences with ghosts, space-faring entities, time travelers, and spirit guides as well as your own existence on other planets, in other dimensions, and in the past and future.

To the degree that you judge it safe, you can remember and even judiciously share your experiences with other Contactors as well as people in the ET-experiencers' networks. You can, of course, share under a pen name and keep your privacy.

I suggest you let yourself remember such experiences. You can opt to keep your contacts private or share them. You learn, when you follow the cues below, to review and relive your contacts from your Center. Then you choose what to tell and what to hide from those who might freak if they hear what you experienced.

The cues teach you to center yourself, to identify with your Center. Your Center is your conscious awareness of your many sub-selves or inner voices. From your ever-expanding Center, you coordinate behavior that meets the deep needs of ever more of your inner voices.

Your Center takes into account the needs of your Contactor sub-self as well as the needs of your primary social and practical selves. Primary selves like your Pleaser, Intellect, Parent, Judge, and Self-Critic may keep you from the full awareness of the Contactor part of you so you can meet your social duties and not sound like a crazy to other people.

From your Center, you choose the degree to which you reveal or conceal your Contactor sub-self and its unconventional experiences. You assess how much of your Contactor you reveal to your own awareness and to other people.

From your Center you can assess probable push-back you'll get if you remember and share your contacts. You predict possible push-back from mates, friends, bosses, disinformation agents, military intimidators, religious bigots, and people who fear your revelations.

Such people may fear your revelations if they've repressed their own paranormal intimations. You decide how much to reveal and how much to conceal, but you can at least let yourself remember.

The cue sequence below begins with an evocation of your primary inner voices. Seek their permission to explore your Contactor. The primary voices that protect you from shame and punishment may've blocked you from either recalling your contacts or may have blocked you from recalling that you consented to contact.

You must get permission from your protective primary voices to let you hear the memories, desires, and needs of your Inner Contactor. In the cue-sequence, you tell your primary voices you'll let them stop interviewing your Contactor if these they sense that you're recalling too much too fast. Your protective voices let you remember enough for you to handle as you respond to the cues to follow.

CREATE SETTING WHERE YOU CAN EMOTE LOUDLY

Disconnect phone, make sure no one can interrupt you for a few hours as you work through the cues. You'll need several chairs or cushions and an area large enough area to lie down. Wear loose-fitting clothes. Create semi-darkness in the room.

VET A CUE-READER OR EXPLORE IN PRIVATE

Ask a nonjudgmental friend or therapist – your Reader
– to read the cues to you. Tell her or him to give you
plenty of time – at least five deep breaths – to respond
to each cue. Make sure the reader doesn't challenge
the reality status (ontology) of your contact memories
or ask questions that imply answers s/he expects.

If you lack an open-minded reader, read the cues
aloud into a recording device and play them to yourself.
Or read each cue to yourself and take as much time as
you like to respond aloud or in writing.

INSTRUCTIONS FOR THE READER:

1) Read the cues in bold aloud to the experiencer.
2) Exception: read words in square brackets [like this]
silently. The person to whom you read is "the
Experiencer."

3) Give the experiencer a few breaths of time to
respond aloud where you see asterisks (***). If the
experiencer doesn't respond to a cue-sentence, pause
several breaths and read the cue aloud again.

4) Address the Experiencer's inner voices and the
entities s/he invokes respectfully, appreciatively: do
not push their limits.

[Start here, read aloud:]

["Center Yourself" Visualization]

Sit here [Indicate place]**: it's the place for you to center yourself where you hear all your inner voices (parts). I'll address your Center with your name** [example: "Alex" is the name of my Center].

Breathe deeply and center yourself.

Tell me, Center, about one of the main protective inner voices (like Intellect, Critic, Pleaser, and Pusher) you present to the world. What words or labels do you use for that voice? [Example: I call my Primary **"Professor Lessin"**] ***

Describe this primary voice, the one you call [Use the same word Experiencer did to label the Primary]. **Say what this Primary is like and what it does for you.** ***

Thank you, Center.

["Identify with a Primary Sub-self" Visualization]

Dis-identify with your Center and move to a new place to embody this Primary; a sub-self from which you relate to other people. ***

[Wait till Experiencer moves. when you read the cues, substitute the name (e.g. Inner Critic) with which Experiencer "Primary" where you see the word "Primary" below].

Hi. Embody that Primary.   Say who you are [an example, you'd say, "Embody your Critic and say who you are."] **and the job you do in your Experiencer's ecology. *****

When, Primary, did your life start? How long have you been around? What's your history as [Experiencer name]**'s Primary? *****

Say, Primary, what voices you protect. ***

What contributions have you, as [Experiencer name]'s **Primary, made to** [Experiencer's name] **throughout life? *****

What would you like to be acknowledged and appreciated for? ***

When I'll ask you, Primary, to let [Experiencer's name] **speak from an inner voice that accesses E.T.s, ghosts, multi-dimensionals, visions, dreams, and/or simultaneous existences in other times and places, if you sense your person's Inner Child panic, shift the Contactor voice offstage and again take center-stage in Experiencer's consciousness. Ok, begin now. *****

**Thank you, Primary. I liked talking with you. Now
let** [Experiencer's name] **return to the Center
position.**

["Return to Center" Visualization]

[Wait till Experiencer moves.] **Hello again, Center.
Say what you learned about the primary voice you
just embodied.** ***

**Tell me, Center, about your Contactor, an inner
sub-self–that experiences the paranormal.** ***

Move your seat to a new place for your Contactor.

[Embody Contactor]

[Wait till Experiencer moves.] **Become your
Contactor. As Contactor, say what name your
person can call you.** ***

[Example: what I call my contactor
"Alexander-Ben-Irving." use Experiencer's name for
the word "Contractor" wherever you see it in the cues].

Say, Contactor, how you are, what you do for
[Experiencer's name] **and what you like.** ***

["Contact Events" Visualization]

Tell me, Contactor, and main contact events with E.T.s, ghosts, multi- dimensionals, visions, dreams and/or simultaneous existences in other times and places in this and other lives with [Experiencer's name]. ***

Relate one critical contact event in this life, a past life or future life. ***

["Trance Induction Steps" Visualization]

Imagine, Contactor, you descend ten steps of a spiral stairway. Each time you exhale, slide your hand along the banister, go down a step and relax more. [Pause] **after a while, step off of the staircase and onto a landing.**

You see a blackboard and chalk on the landing. Take the chalk and write a number on the blackboard corresponding to how relaxed you are, with the numbers 1-12 as slightly relaxed, 13-24 as moderately relaxed, 25 plus as very relaxed. Tell me the number you write on the blackboard. ***

Relax more by writing the next number in the sequence below the first one. ***

Relax still more by writing the next number behind the first one. ***

Write the next number above your initial number, and relax more. ***

Deepen your relaxation: write the next number in front of the first one. What number do you write in front? ***

["Elevator-Transporter" Visualization]

Opposite the blackboard, see an elevator which is also a transporter. Its dial shows you're on a floor, numbered the same as how many years old you are now. Enter the elevator-transporter.

Push one of the elevator buttons. The floor number on the button you push is the year to which you'll descend to access a critical event that might make your person's contact experiences more accessible to conscious awareness. What's the number of the button you pushed? ***

Go down in the elevator to the floor/age of the button you pushed. If your person experienced the event in a past life, let the elevator go to the subterranean floors of the building. If s/he experienced the event in a parallel or dream world existence, let him, or her enter the transporter chamber under the building, activate the transporter, and emerge in an alternate reality.

["Relive Critical Contact Experience" Visualization]

Emerge from the elevator or transporter and step into a hall. There, see many doors. One bears your name and the contact experience that will help you remember so your Center can access your contacts.

Open the door to your critical contact experience. Go inside a holographic chamber that can let you relive the experience. Anytime, you can shift to a neutral, witnessing mode, detached from emotion or you can let a primary sub-self take you from this reverie if it is too intense for you right now.

If you choose to proceed, see, hear, feel, sense and intuit everyone and everything as it was when you first experienced it.

Use the present (is, am, are) tense and describe the contact you relive. Experience and say:

"What I see ..." ***

"What I hear..." ***

"What I feel..." ***

"What I smell... " ***

"What I taste..."***

"What I sense..." ***

"What I think..." ***

"What I intuit..." ***

How do you breathe during this situation? ***

Do you get an implant, upgrade, pregnancy, healing during the experience. ***

Do you give ova, sperm or a fetus in the experience? ***

[Speak as "Other" & Other's Commander]

Now let "other" (one of the beings or people present or implied in the experience) speak with your voice, but not take you over. Temporarily identify with and vocalize for the "Other" in your paranormal experience. [Allow plenty of time; take 10 breaths before you read the next cue]. *** *** ***

Who are you, Being, who now will speak with [Experiencer's name]'s voice? ***
What are your reasons for contacting [Experiencer's name]? ***

What mission do you have for [Experiencer's name]? ***

How does your contact with [Experiencer's name] fit into a program? ***

What's the purpose of the implant, upgrading or manipulation of the Contactee's reproductive material and organs? ***

What's your existence and the existence of your colleagues like in space, time, on your Homeworld, or in your dimension? ***

How is your Homeworld organized? How is it organized politically? ***

Describe housing, family and social relations on your Homeworld. Tell me about transport devices and craft there. ***

Cross-connect with your Headquarters. We wish to speak with your High Commander. [Allow time] ***

Commander, tell us your purpose contacting my Experiencer. ***

What larger mission do you have for contactors in general and for my Experience in particular? ***

Thank you, Commander. Now let your subordinate–the one we're calling "Other"– resume speaking through [Experiencer's name]'s voice.

As the voice of the "Other," what else would you like your person to know before you release her/his vocal apparatus? ***

Thank you, "Other."

[Embody Contactor Again]

Return again to the seat for your Contactor.

[Wait till Experiencer moves back to the place where s/he enacts Contactor]

Hello again, Contactor. Tell your person what you'd like to be appreciated for now and through the years. ***

What do you want, Contactor? ***

Why do you want that? What needs motivate what you want? ***

What else would you like your person to know before s/he goes back to Center? ***

Bid adieu to your Contactor for now. Exit the hologram room, return to the elevator- transporter in the building of your ages. Go back in the elevator-transporter to the floor of your current age.

**Go past the blackboard where you chalked the
numbers, then ascend the stairs that lead you
back to right here. On the tenth steps from the top,
feel your consciousness start to return to the
present. Step 9, more awake. 8,7,6, 5, becoming
more awake. 4, 3, 2–almost totally alert. 1–wake up,
fully awake and alert.**

[Snap your fingers; give Experiencer time to re-orient.]

[Return to Center]

**Welcome back.   Move back to the place for your
Center.** [Wait till s/he moves]

**As Center, what did you learn from accessing your
contactor and the voice of the "other" and its
commander that your paranormal voice channeled
for you? *****

[Identify with Neutral Witness]

**Stand behind me and become neutral. Witness the
energy from each of the positions–the Primary's,
Contactor's, and other voices' seats–from which
you spoke as I summarize what each said. Feel the
energy of each as I review them for you.**

[Synopsize what Experiencer said from each voice].
###

[Return to Center]

Experience yourself between your Primary and your Contactor. With the info from your Witness on your current ecology, regulate how much of your Contactor's experience to reveal and what to conceal in various social contexts. Comment on the balance that seems right for you now. ***

[Own Your Power]

Pull your energy back from me: realize you now know how to conduct this sort of exploration on your own, without my reading to you.

<u>References for this Regression Protocol:</u>

Lamb, B., 2016, "Extra-Terrestrial Contact Experiences: How Regression Therapy Can Help" the Journal of Regression Therapy

Lessin, S. and J. 1998 – present, ExtraterrestrialContact.com

Stone, H. & Winkelman, S., 1998, "Embracing Our Selves," and "Embracing Each Other" both 1989, New World Library: San Rafael).

ABOUT THE AUTHOR

KEN JOHNSTON SR

Ken Johnston Sr was one of four Civilian Astronaut Consultant Pilots from the NASA Apollo Moon Program.

Ken is a retired aerospace worker, served as a US Marine, and is a well-known NASA Whistleblower. Ken is well known because he was a witness to history, to NASA image manipulation, and he saved an archive of early Apollo-era photos that are original to the time before NASA digitized and created an on-line database of images.

Johnston used a loophole in the orders he was given to destroy five sets of 8"X10" glossy photo prints from the Apollo program. When he worked in the Data and Photo Control Lab in Houston during the moon missions, he saved a set for his own records.

His archive is prized by researchers and lunar anomaly hunters because it has been discovered that there has been an intentional, systematic, physical and digital manipulation of NASA imagery and media in order to cover up what was found on the moon and recorded in film and photos by the Apollo astronauts.

www.ingramcontent.com/pod-product-compliance
Lightning Source LLC
Chambersburg PA
CBHW070125260726
48658CB00001B/263